The Way It Was
BACK THEN

*To
Brice Marsh
My Friend*

Best Wishes & God Bless

Robert Earl Woodard

The Way It Was
BACK THEN

SHORT STORIES FROM A COUNTRY BOY

ROBERT EARL WOODARD

TATE PUBLISHING
AND ENTERPRISES, LLC

Published by Tate Publishing & Enterprises, LLC
127 E. Trade Center Terrace | Mustang, Oklahoma 73064 USA
1.888.361.9473 | www.tatepublishing.com

Tate Publishing is committed to excellence in the publishing industry. The company reflects the philosophy established by the founders, based on Psalm 68:11,
"The Lord gave the word and great was the company of those who published it."

Book design copyright © 2014 by Tate Publishing, LLC. All rights reserved.
Cover design by Rtor Maghuyop
Interior design by Jomar Ouano

Published in the United States of America

ISBN: 978-1-63063-874-0
1. Biography & Autobiography / Personal Memoirs
2. Biography & Autobiography / Historical
14.03.05

Annie Mae and Roy Chester "Buster" Woodard (my parents) days before Dad shipped out for World War II.

Dedication

I would like to dedicate this book to my parents, Roy Chester "Buster" Woodard and Annie Mae Woodard. I want to thank them for setting good examples, teaching the importance of God, family, and the value of hard work. The way they lived their lives set an example for our family, and their wisdom and advice have been cherished down through the generations.

Acknowledgments

I would like to thank my family and friends for their support while I was writing my first book. A special thanks to my wife, Sharon; my children, Deanna and Matt; my brother, Jerry; and my cousin, Abbie Turner Wiersma with Presentations Etc. Studio.

Contents

Introduction

Hard work, adventure, and excitement describe the way it was back when I was growing up. Running barefoot in the fields, going through the woods, swimming in the river, and pulling big catfish from the river were our entertainment. Homemade biscuits and homegrown food cooked on the wood stove were our way of life—and something I will not forget. It was a way of survival that had been handed down through the generations. Many changes occurred during my lifetime. With all the modern conveniences of today, we look back and say, "Those were the good old days." Maybe we say that because life was so simple back then. Sitting on the front porch after dark, listening to stories from our parents and grandparents created many great memories. Now, it is my turn to share my memories with others.

Annie Mae Woodard (my mother) and Rob "Papa" Woodard (her father-in-law), in the cotton field, during World War II.

I Know You Can, but I Don't Want to See You Kill a Good Mule Doing It

On our farm as a young boy, plowing a mule all day was an everyday thing in the spring and summer. We had several mules during this time. Mules that did not work out for whatever reason did not stay on our farm long. They had to earn their keep. We had two mules that withstood the test, Charlie and Duke. Charlie was a slow, steady mule that was easy to plow. Duke was a high-stepping big red mule that could really move along and plow all day long. As the day went on, it seemed that he sensed we were about to finish and would get faster, or maybe it was because by the end of the day, I was worn down.

So one day, we asked my dad if we could buy a TV. My dad told us, "If you want a TV, we can rent Mr. Blackwood's five acres of cotton ground across the road, and if we make five bales, we can buy a TV in the fall." So we rented the five acres of land to plant cotton, so that we could buy a TV. This was in addition to the cotton we planted on our land. We never had a TV before, but we wanted one because in order to see a TV, we would have to go visit a neighbor's house to watch one. People did make a point to visit a lot more back in those days. This seemed like a good, sure way of getting a TV. It would take lots of work, but we were used to that. So we rented the land.

We plowed the field and prepared the ground. We planted the cotton and got a good stand. We were blessed with good weather that year. We had to hoe and chop the cotton to thin it out, which took several days. We plowed the cotton using a faller plow, which was a plow that had two fenders that would run along beside the cotton and throw the dirt away from it which made it easy for chopping and hoeing. After working the cotton several times, it was looking very promising. As time passed, the cotton got bigger and started growing well.

It was hot in late June of that year, and the cotton was now knee-high. It was time to lay the cotton by, meaning fertilizing around the cotton using a fertilizer distributor, hoeing the cotton for the last time and throwing the dirt to the row using a scratcher gangplow. You would do this by going up and down each side of each row to put the dirt to the cotton, or in those days, the saying was: "round the row." To plow five acres of cotton going "round the row" was unheard of in those days.

The day came to put the dirt to the cotton using the scratcher gang, and I chose old Duke to pull the scratcher to get the job done. I got up early, watered and fed the mules, and I put the collar and hangs on old Duke. I hooked the plowing harness up and headed for the field. I was there by daylight. The man we rented the land from was in his seventies, and had planted cotton in that field for many years. After plowing for a while that morning, he came down to see how I was doing, and I said, "Okay." I told him that I was going to plow the entire field and lay the cotton by today. He said, "No one has ever plowed this field round the row in one day." I said, "They didn't have Duke."

Mr. Blackwood was a man that admired good mules, and he knew that I had a good mule in Duke. He said, "Don't get Duke too hot," then he walked on. The sun was beaming down, the air was blowing across my face, but we never stopped. At each end of the row, Duke would heed the command *geehaw*. The dirt was plowing well, and we did not stop until I could step on the shadow of my own head. That meant it was close to midday. I went to a nearby spring, watered Duke, and got a drink for myself from the spring as I had done many times, then it was right back to the plowing. By midafternoon, going on nine hours of plowing, the sun began to sink low, but it was still very hot and there was not a dry thread on me. Duke was also lathered up from sweat. I was down at the lower side of the field with one terrace to go when I looked up the hill, and saw Mr. Blackwood coming down the edge of the field with his mule. I stopped at the end of the row to meet him. I said, "What are you doing down here?" He said, "I am going to help you finish." I said, "Mr. Blackwood, I am going to finish before dark." He said, "I know you can, but I don't want to see you kill a good mule doing it." He started at the lower side and met me halfway up on the last terrace. That is how people would help you out in those days. He did not charge a penny. He also had feeling for Duke because he loved mules.

Once it was ready, we had to pick the cotton, put it on a truck, and take it to the gin. We had to decide if we wanted to sell the cotton or store it in a warehouse and wait for prices to go up. It all worked out that prices were good then, so we sold our cotton, but we did not make five bales. We made eight bales: the best cotton that was ever made in that field. I guess it was meant to be because we bought our RCA black-and-white television that fall. It was amazing how well they made televisions back then. We watched that black-and-white television for years, and it never went bad. Many years later when color television came out, we all wished it would tear up so we could get a color television.

The mules grew old but left many memories on the farm. It was a way of life, but soon, cotton was no longer king, and other crops would replace it. Tractors would replace the mules, and it would be the end of an era that would never be returned to. Things also changed for me. I left the cotton fields to pursue another dream: to get my education from Auburn University. After receiving my degree in education, I continued farming. Years later, I was mowing the hay off that farm in an air-conditioned tractor, remembering as a boy the hot days of walking behind that mule all day long. I never dreamed as a boy following a mule that an air-conditioned tractor would exist. It is amazing how things change.

What a great lesson my Dad taught me that year about working and earning what I wanted, because when you work for it and earn it, you value it much more. Also, the lesson from the old gentleman on how to help thy neighbor is why we can now look back and say that those were the good old days.

This is the boat featured in "Be Careful of Jersey Bulls and Muddy Water, for Both are Dangerous." It still floats on my lake today.

Be Careful of Jersey Bulls and Muddy Water, for Both Are Dangerous

As a young boy, my friends and I had many adventures roaming the woods and rivers in this county. We escaped danger many times because we had no fear. My elderly neighbor was like my grandpa. He was famous for his words of wisdom that always had a lot of meaning. He used to tell me, "Son, be careful of Jersey bulls and muddy water—for both are dangerous." That saying sparked my interest because I wanted to ride a Jersey bull. (I later did, and yes, I got bucked off and bruised). We also knew we could catch big catfish out of the muddy water on the Warrior River after a big rain.

One day after a hard day's work, it came a big rain. We decided we would head for the river. Usually, we would catch our own bait, either by seining minnows or catching them in minnow baskets. On some occasions, we would fiddle worms up. You would do this by going into the woods, cutting a small tree down, and sawing back and forth on the top, causing a vibrating sound. This vibration would cause the worms to crawl up out of the ground. However, on this fishing trip, we did not have time to catch the bait, so we bought two dollars' worth of minnows from the minnow farm and headed to the river. I did not know that on this day I would lose the two dollars' worth of minnows I had bought for fish bait.

We loaded our twelve-foot fishing boat and headed for the river, to a well-known place that held many big catfish called Scirum Bluff. We had been there many times before and had caught lots of fish. On this trip, we invited my future father-in-law to go with us. It was his first time to go with us, and as usual, he was dressed in his heavy boots and overalls.

Scirum Bluff was also the favorite swimming hole for many because it had deep water, sandy shores, and a high bluff to dive off (which I had done on several occasions). But the purpose of this trip was not to swim but to catch big catfish. On many trips, we caught so many fish that one person could barely carry them. However, this trip would be our most memorable trip of all.

The rains came, we had the bait and the trotlines, and now, it was time to put the lines in our favorite places. From experience, we knew to put the trotlines on the shoals in the swift water, which was how you caught the most fish. With lines in place and the river on the rise and turning muddy, it seemed like the perfect setting to catch the big one. Little did we know it had rained a lot harder up the river than we had thought. After an hour of work, the lines were in place. Right before dark is the best time to put the bait on the hooks. The first line was baited with ease, as was the second, but the third line would be a little tricky. It was at the lower end of the Scirum hole, right above the rapids where the water was forced over the rapids in a small area. We had put trotlines in this place several times before in the past, but the river was rising fast, and the water was turning muddy. We had to get the trotlines baited, for it was a good place to catch big fish. Two of us must hold on to the trotline in the rapidly moving water to keep the boat from going into the forceful rapids. We had always done this with two people in the boat, but this time, we had three. The extra weight and the force of the water created a tough challenge. Two of us were holding the line at each end of the boat, but my friend's line slipped from his hand. The boat spun around with the force of the water. It was too great of a force for me to hold onto the line, and I had to let go.

That was all it took for an exciting ride down a long rapid to the next hole. I was in the front of the boat, trying to keep my boat from hitting the big rocks as we went down the rapids. Knowing the river, I knew we had to miss some big rocks at the lower end of the rapids. Positioning the boat and paddling as hard as I could, we missed the big rocks. I was so excited about the accomplishment and the fact that the boat was still upright, and I was feeling really good about making it all the way down the rapids in one piece—that is until I saw at the bottom of the rapids that the water was going down and boiling back over the top of itself like a big wave in the ocean. We had no time for any adjustments, and then we hit the swell. The boat went down in the dip, and the water spilled over into the front of the boat. The boat was half-filled with water, and suddenly, it disappeared from under us and was gone. We were left to survive the rapidly moving water without a boat. All of my swimming skills and instincts took over. I thought of saving my remaining two dollars of minnows, and I grabbed the minnow bucket. It was hard to swim in rapid water with a five-gallon bucket of minnows over my head and not spill them, but I almost got them to shore when I heard a yell: "I need some help!" I looked back to see my friend holding my future father-in-law up by his overall galluses going down the river. Being young, I did not realize that an older man in his boots and overalls could not swim as well as we could. Letting the bucket of minnows go, I swam as hard as I could to him, grabbing one of the galluses and pulling him up. My friend was holding the other gallus. We swam to shore pulling him by his overalls. With him safe on the bank— which was not an easy task—and with his overalls and heavy boots full of water, I saw my boat surface going down the river.

Since this was my only boat, I had to try to save it. I ran down to the river bank, jumped in and swam to my boat. However, it was impossible to pull the boat out of the rapidly moving water. The boat was approaching the next rapid. The currents were so strong that the boat and I both went over the next rapid. At that point, all I could do was hang on for the ride. The boat was now in the next hole, and I was trying to pull it to the bank. The current in the water began to slow, and it washed me close enough to the bank that I was able to grab some limbs and pull the boat out onto the bank. We were all safe, and our boat had no holes. (Still to this day, I use this boat as a fishing boat on my own lake.) I realized that I had lost the rest of my minnows, my big spotlight, and Bowie knife. The rains came that night and washed all our trotlines away, so we did not catch a fish that night for all of our trouble.

A week later, after the river cleared up and after diving in fifteen feet of water, I was able to recover my spotlight. However, I never could find my Bowie knife, and the minnows were gone.

This was one of our adventures on the river, which, at that time, we thought was just another day of fishing on the river with some excitement. I am glad we had that day for the memories, but thinking back on it, I realize now how fortunate we were that everything turned out okay. I know now that I am older that my elderly neighbor knew what he was talking about when he said, "Be careful of Jersey bulls and muddy water, for both are dangerous."

The author, approximately ten years
old, playing in his yard.

The Dreams

Everyone has to have a dream to look forward to in life. It did not take me long in my young life to find out that you have to work to make your dreams come true. Things were very different in my childhood days than they are today. The things that children take for granted now, we had to work for. In my life, my dreams have gone from being very small dreams to very big dreams. As a small boy, I would dream about going to the store, which was about a quarter of a mile below my house, to get a Coke. In order to fulfill that dream, I would have to find five Coke bottles along the side of the road so that I could take them to the store and get the deposit on the bottles to buy my Coke. That childhood lesson taught me about how to work to make dreams come true.

Of course, I always dreamed about hunting and fishing and catching that big catfish or bass, or bagging game for my Granny Woodard to cook to put food on the table. ("Bagging game" was hunting squirrels, rabbits, and sometimes quails, as this was a part of our everyday life.) As time passed, I fulfilled other dreams such as playing quarterback on my high school football team, and again,

I had to do the work to acquire the necessary skills to fulfill that dream.

As I grew older, I begin to have different dreams that I did not think about earlier in my life. While working in the fields plowing cotton and corn, I used to dream about having a cattle farm with a house on a hill with a big lake. As a high school senior, I had a dream of being an agriculture teacher because I liked my agriculture teacher and thought that would be a great job to have since I loved farming. A goal that we had in agriculture class was trying to complete the requirements needed to receive the Future Farmer of America Award. Completing this goal was a very valuable lesson for me on how to conquer obstacles and fulfill a dream because it was a great deal of work in order to obtain this award.

There were many requirements to fulfill in order to obtain this award. One of the requirements was to plant an acre of corn and have it yield one hundred bushels of corn on one acre. In order to do this, I knew that I would have to put a lot of care into this corn patch. I pulled a soil sample to see what fertilizers were needed. I plowed up the land and planted the seeds. I worked that corn patch and gave full attention to every detail because I wanted to achieve my dream of receiving the Future Farmer of America Award. In addition, we had to keep a notebook that logged all of our activities and costs in making the corn.

As it turned out, my corn patch yielded over one hundred bushels of corn, and I was very proud when I received that award. Working toward the goal of receiving this award helped to teach me something that my dad had already told me, which is that you can't get anywhere in life if you do not work for it. That was a lesson that my dad constantly instilled in me, and it was one of the most important things he taught me about life. If you have a dream and work at it hard enough, most of the time you will reach that dream. You may not reach every dream, but that doesn't mean you stop trying; you just start reaching for another dream. Like the game of football, you may not win every game, but you have to get ready to try to win the next game.

I also thought a lot of my football coach and had dreams of growing up to be like him. I loved playing football and being the quarterback on the team, and I had dreams of how great it would be to coach. I did not study much in high school because there was a lot of work to do on the farm, but I still made good grades. By my senior year, I realized that I had to do all the work, including school work, which was necessary for me to reach my big dreams of being a teacher and maybe a coach. Both my football coach and agriculture teacher had made a positive influence on me, and they had motivated me to go on to college. I also picked the right girlfriend to help me along the path of pursuing my dream to become a teacher, as she was also planning on making a teacher.

My senior year, I found out that we had to take the ACT test in order to get into college. When I first heard of the ACT test, my thought was that we would go and let someone observe us to see if we acted okay before they let us into college. I was soon told that we would be taking a test like we had never taken before. After taking the test, I learned that was so right. I was so happy after finding out I scored one point over the requirement to get into Auburn University. Now, I needed a plan for how I was going to pay my way through Auburn.

I would need to farm one year in order to make enough money to go to Auburn. So in the spring of my senior year of high school, I planted sixty acres of produce. I worked hard all summer, gathering produce and going to the farmers' market to sell it. I saved my money so that I could attend Snead State Junior College that fall. My girlfriend attended the University of Alabama that summer after we graduated high school. She was not happy in Tuscaloosa, so she moved back home, and we both started to Snead in the fall of 1970. I got a job driving a bus for Snead State Junior College, which paid for my tuition. I also got a part-time job at an egg house, loading eggs onto big trucks in the afternoons and at night. I left for my bus route at six in the morning. I would get to school by seven thirty and have classes until one. I would study in the library till three and be home by four every day. Then it would be time to go to work at the egg house. Between school and work, I stayed very busy.

I got married to my high school girlfriend on November 7, 1970 at Corinth Baptist Church. After we got married, we moved to Boaz, Alabama, which is near Snead College where we were attending school. After we moved to Boaz, I gave up my bus route to get a job, making five dollars per hour handling twelve-inch cement blocks on the construction site of a big church. This was some very tough work. Back in those days, we handed the twelve-inch blocks up to the block mason, who laid the block and applied the mortar. We had no heavy machinery to move the blocks. Instead, we would get them to the block mason by handing them up a series of scaffolds until we were several scaffolds high. The block mason wanted every block handed to him so that all he had to do was place the block in the wall and put mortar around it. During this time, the contractor fired about fifteen boys, and several more quit. One other boy and I were the only two block movers that stayed until the church was finished. Although it was very tough work, this was the most money I had ever made per hour up to this point in my life. At this time, the minimum wage was $2.25 per hour. At $5.00 per hour, I thought I was really making the big-time money. I stayed with this job until late spring, when the church was finished.

In the spring of 1971, my wife and I moved back home to the farm. We moved into an apartment in Blountsville. We didn't ride the bus to school this summer, but instead, we drove to Snead to take our classes. We farmed during the summer of 1971, just as we had done the year before. We rented some of our neighbors' land to farm on, and my dad also let us plant produce on some of his land. We also helped my dad farm. It was some long and hard hours, but I enjoyed it, and I now had my wife to help me.

During this time, we never missed taking a full load in college. I had hoped to hit it big on some produce patches so that we would have enough money to go to Auburn when we finished our time at Snead Junior College. When we finished farming that summer, we had two thousand dollars in the bank, which was a good bit of money in those days. My wife and I thought we had enough money to fulfill our dreams of going to

Auburn to get our teaching degrees, so we put this into a savings account.

In the fall of 1971, we attended Snead, and I got a full-time job at the egg house in Blountsville. My job was to help a man clean up the mess of broken and rotten eggs that was made during the day shift when they processed and packed the eggs. By six every morning, our job was to have the egg house spotless. It was a tough and messy job. I would come in, take a shower, eat breakfast, and be at school by eight. We would usually stay at school all day in class or studying in the library. We would try to be home by four or five o'clock so that I could get some sleep before ten. I would usually sleep until nine thirty and then get up and go to work, where I earned sixty dollars per week. One night, the man I was working with fell and broke his leg. After a few nights of doing the cleaning alone, the owner walked in one morning and asked if I could do the job myself, or if he needed to get someone to help me. I told him I could do the job myself, but if I did the work of two people, I should get paid for two. He did not reply and walked on through the plant. When I picked my paycheck up that week, it was doubled. The owner continued to pay me double until the man returned to work. I will never forget that.

We finished our two-year degree at Snead Junior College in the spring of '72. We were Auburn bound and ready to enroll at Auburn University for the summer quarter. However, we needed to find a place to live first. After looking at some apartments, we decided we could not afford them and determined that a mobile home purchased and placed on a lot would be the cheapest way to go. So we found a new mobile home for $4,500. All we needed then was to figure out how to buy it. The interest rate and payment from the mobile home company were way too high, and besides, they would not sell a home to a person with no job or credit. I asked my father-in-law to borrow the money, and he told me to go to the bank. My dad also advised me to go to the bank to try to establish some credit. So I went to the same bank where I had put my money into a savings account. I walked into the president's office and asked him to borrow $4,500. He said, "How much do you want to put down?" Then I said, "Nothing because I need the money I have to live on and pay tuition while attending school at Auburn University." He looked at the secretary and said, "Write them a check for forty-five hundred dollars, set the payments up on low interest, and make the payments come due yearly at the end of the year. They can pay whatever they can afford to pay, and if they are in school, they can just pay the interest on the money." I did not have to have anyone to cosign with me. I just borrowed the money with my signature and my word that I would pay him back. I will never forget that day at the bank and how it was so vital to us at that time of our lives in trying to fulfill our dreams. To this day, I am still very appreciative of the man who was president of that bank.

After moving to Auburn, I got a job at the vet school in the pathology department. After I worked there a few days, I found out why I got the job—no one else wanted that job because you had to have a tough stomach and a lot of grit to work there. While working there, I came in contact with a raccoon that had rabies. I was sent to get shots which made me very sick. However, after I recovered, I continued working at the vet school part-time, putting in fifteen hours a week while taking a full load of classes. After taxes, I brought home twenty-seven dollars per week. Our rent for the lot where we parked our mobile home was only eighteen dollars per month, and our groceries were just ten dollars per week. Our parents helped us out with food from the farm, and we made it just fine.

After one quarter at Auburn, I changed my major from agriculture education to physical education with the dream of teaching physical education and coaching—a decision that I am still happy with today. Auburn had some of the toughest classes I had ever attended, but the challenges just made me more determined to meet the demands of my instructors. People that thought physical education at Auburn was going to be easy were wrong, because I watched students drop out or fail every day. I had friends to make it all the way to the upper-level classes of Kinesiology and The Organization and Administration of Health, Physical Education, and Recreation, yet never be able to pass those classes and have to drop out. I actually made better grades at Auburn than I did in high school. One of my friends made a comment to me after staying up all night studying for two nights in a row that it was hard. I looked at him and said, "This is not hard. Have you ever plowed a mule from sunup till sundown? Now that's hard! This is easy compared to following a mule all day!"

At Auburn, our life was totally different than back home on the farm, but all the principles of hard work were the same. We were having fun going to football games, fishing, attending classes, and studying when we needed to. We met many new friends and several special people that helped us along the way. I saw a lot of people go home because they failed out of Auburn, but I was determined to do the work needed in order to reach my dream. I found out that to be successful at Auburn, I had to apply the same work habits in class as I did back on the farm. It was like planting that corn patch; you had to put every effort into it and work very hard in every class to be successful. I knew that being successful in my schoolwork was necessary in order to make my dreams a reality.

After catching a lot of seven and eight pound bass, meeting some tough challenges in classes, being exposed to rabies at the vet school, and almost getting blown away in a tornado, my wife and I were looking forward to graduating at the end of the fall quarter of 1973 right before Christmas. But in the summer of 1973, before I graduated, a friend on the Auburn coaching staff asked, "Do you want a job coaching at Lee Academy?" He said, "I am going to recommend you for the job." I had become best friends with one of the coaches on the Auburn football staff. He was a great guy, and his wife was super nice. I will always be appreciative of their help and their friendship at Auburn. These were the kind of good people you usually met at Auburn. I went for the job interview, walked in, and talked with the head coach five minutes and he said, "You have the job. It pays sixty dollars per week, and you will be the assistant football coach, head junior high basketball coach, and start our first-ever baseball team in the spring and serve as head coach." What some nice words to hear! I couldn't believe I had a job before I graduated.

I graduated with my bachelor's degree at the end of fall quarter 1973 and continued working on my masters in physical education while coaching at Lee Academy during the winter and spring quarters of 1974. However, before I could get into graduate school, I had to take the GRE. Taking this test was something I never thought I would be doing, and I will never forget how difficult the daylong exam was. I look back and remember taking the ACT test, and I can tell you that the GRE was much, much harder than the ACT test. I'll always remember it said in the instructions not to guess because any incorrect answer would be counted off twice as much as an unanswered question. They only wanted you to answer the questions you knew. I read the first seventeen questions and did not know the answer to a single question, so I had to guess. I suppose I guessed well enough because I passed! I was accepted into graduate school, and I felt like I had really accomplished and learned a lot since being at Auburn. I remember the words from my high school principal saying, "Get a degree from Auburn University, and you will have something you can be proud of."

In the fall of 1974, I got a job teaching and coaching football, basketball, and track at Oneonta City School, which was located in Blount County where I grew up. We returned to Auburn for summer school in the summers of 1975 and 1976 to finish my master's degree. I received my masters in physical education at the end of the summer quarter of 1976. It was also a feeling of great accomplishment because I had worked and paid my own way through college for both my bachelor's and master's degrees. It goes back to what my dad said many times: "If you work for it and earn it, you will value it a lot more." That was so true!

With a baby on the way, we moved our mobile home back to the farm in Blount County where we started our teaching careers. Our dreams of teaching and coaching had become a reality. We built our house on the hill like I had always dreamed of, and we moved in a week before Christmas in 1976. We also started farming again in 1977, raising cattle and produce while teaching. A few years later, we built the big lake by my house. The dream about the house, farm, cattle, and big lake had come true. But the dream now is to write this book. I never really thought I would be writing a book but I am! I am living out that dream as well, getting to share my stories with others.

The Calf Called Houdini

It was a normal day on the farm on that spring morning until about eight o'clock. I heard a cow bawling. I walked toward the bawling cow, suspecting she had lost her calf. As I got closer to her, I realized she was standing on the edge of a bluff looking down, possibly looking for her calf. Along the back side of the pasture is a one hundred to one hundred fifty foot bluff down to the Locust Fork of the Warrior River. When I got to the cow, I looked off the bluff, and there I found a major problem, a three-hundred-pound calf standing about seventy-five feet down on a ledge. The calf was trapped on a ledge that was about twenty feet wide and sixty feet long with no way to escape. Below the ledge, the bluff dropped another thirty feet straight to the river.

The river was high due to heavy rains, and the water was moving with great force. The only way to the ledge was to go up the river about three hundred yards, then down to the river, walk back down the river to the ledge, and climb the thirty-foot bluff to the ledge to where the calf was standing. There was no way to rescue this calf, except to pull the calf straight up the bluff the way he went down. Realizing I needed some help, I went to my mother's house and asked my brother to help me rescue a calf that was trapped on a ledge down on the bluff. We got several ropes and got the tractor and returned to the ledge. The plan was to tie the calf up with ropes, then tie the ropes to the tractor, and pull the calf straight up the bluff. We soon realized this was not the best idea.

The first problem was catching the calf and getting the rope on him. After twenty minutes trying to lasso the calf, we realized this calf did not want to be caught or rescued. He would run from one side of the ledge to the other to avoid being caught. After many attempts, we finally got the rope on the calf. We made a halter to go on his head, and we tied the rope to a tree to hold him. At this time, we felt fairly confident that we had things under control. We tied the calf's feet together so he could not get up. We planned to tie a long rope to the ropes that held the feet together and pull the calf up feet first with the tractor. The second major problem was that the ropes were not long enough to reach the tractor. We could not get the tractor one bit closer to the bluff because of big trees. Now, I would need a new plan.

I went to the house to get the come-a-long (a come-a-long is a piece of equipment that can hoist heavy objects up off the ground using the rope pulley system). I could tie the come-a-long to a tree and then hoist the calf up off the ledge using this equipment. When I returned to the ledge, my brother and the calf were gone. I yelled, and my brother answered, and then I spotted him down river beside the rapids on the bank, soaking wet. I asked, "What happened?" My brother said, "The calf somehow got the halter off his head. I was trying to hold him, and we both went off the thirty-foot ledge into the river. I held on as long as I could, but when I hit the river, I let go." I asked, "Are you hurt?" He said, "Only a few scratches and bruises." I asked, "Were the calf's legs still tied together when he went into the river?" He said, "Yes." I asked, "Where is the calf?" He replied, "The last time I saw the calf, he was going down the river over the rapids." Well, I figured at that point, with the calf's legs being tied up and going down the river over the rapids—it was "good-bye calf."

We walked down the river to see if we could find the calf. Surprisingly, there he was, standing on the bank without a rope on him. Still, the calf has no way out. The calf is now in a worse position: either we have to get him up a one-hundred foot bluff straight up, or he will have to swim the river. We started walking toward the calf. Unbelievably, he jumps into the river and swims down river. He manages to swim to a big rock right out in the middle of the river. The rock is located right above the Dungeon Falls. Now, he is really in a fix. The water is moving rapidly on each side of the rock. Just below him down river is a waterfall going into a long deep hole called the Dungeon.

We were all in a fix now, and we needed more help and more ropes. I went home to call some friends to assist. We returned to the river, and the calf was still on the big rock. We planned our strategies and placed ropes to rescue the calf. Now, if I could get a rope over his head, it would have been good. I had a rope tied to myself for safety. I worked my way toward the calf, wading and swimming in the swift water toward the rock. I made it to the rock and climbed up on it. I approached the calf and got close, but right before I got ready to lasso the calf, it looked back at me and jumped into the river. Down the river over the Dungeon Falls he went, under the water and out of sight. My friend said, "You can kiss that calf good-bye."

After a long time, it seemed like two or three minutes, the calf came up swimming at the lower end of the Dungeon Hole. Yes, he was alive and swimming to the bank, but now, he was really trapped by the river. Trapped by a bluff one hundred fifty feet high and the river at the upper end, he would now have to go down river one quarter mile where he would be trapped by the river and bluff called the Rock Buster. The only way we could get to the calf was to swim, or go back up the bluff and go down the river to a place where we used to climb down a tree to get to that part of the river. The new plan now was that my brother would climb down the tree to the calf's location, walk it one quarter mile down river to the Rock Buster, make him jump into the river, and swim the length of the Rock Buster which is probably two hundred yards to a place where I would be waiting. I knew of a place down river about a half mile where a trail leads from the highway down to the river. We just might get the calf up the trail to the road.

When my brother got to the calf, he drove the calf down river to the Rock Buster. At this point there was no more river bank to walk on because the water went underneath the rocks. So he forced the calf to jump into the river, and it swam the length of the Rock Buster, a good two hundred yards and then climbed out onto the bank where I was waiting for him. Only then did things begin to go our way. I drove the calf up the trail about a quarter mile to the highway. I walked him up beside the highway three quarters of a mile to the road that led to my house. The calf walked down that road, bawling for his mother, to the pasture where his mother was located. The calf then ran right through the fence like it was not there. By the time I caught up to the calf, he was nursing his mother like nothing ever happened.

By then it was four o'clock, but we had accomplished our task. We went home exhausted. We could barely walk from fatigue. We were bruised and scratched from head to toe. We had not had any food or water all day, so we were glad to sit down for dinner that evening to a wonderful meal that my mother and wife had prepared for us several hours earlier that day. We were so tired we could hardly eat. I will never forget that day, but was so glad it turned out the way it did. I was so tired, but I never thought of giving up on the rescue mission because I was so determined to complete the task and rescue the calf. Our dad had taught us not to give up and quit on something you start. At the table, we were talking about the excitement and challenges we had in rescuing the calf. Mother looked at us and said, "Do y'all realize that y'all are not young boys anymore?" She was so right. Our muscles were so sore we could barely move for several days. The calf was fine, not a scratch on him. The calf—through all of his escapes, from getting the halter off his head, falling into the river with his feet tied together, surviving the rapids, and escaping the waterfall—definitely earned the name "Houdini."

My father, Roy Chester "Buster" Woodard,
with pony "Molly" and mule "Charlie."

The Way It Was Back Then

Each generation seems to have it easier. Even though I had it hard growing up, I had it easier than my father and mother. They had it easier than their father and mother, and so on. I was part of the last generation that had "the simple life." It has been amazing to see the changes that have taken place in only a few short generations, from the time my grandfather bought the family farm that I still live on today until the time that I became an adult.

Papa Woodard (my grandfather) bought the 120-acre farm in 1917 for three hundred dollars. His plan to pay for the farm was to cut the timber with a crosscut saw and hew out crossties by hand with an ax. He sold each finished crosstie for a dime a piece. My father told me that on a good day, Papa could finish six crossties. Although it was very hard work, it earned him sixty cents per day, and back then, hired labor was for only fifty cents per day.

The first thing Papa had to do after buying the farm was to build a house and then clear the land for farming. After cutting the timber in order to prepare the land for farming, he would dig around the stumps and pull the stumps out with mules. Once the stumps were out of the ground, he would pile them up and burn them. After the land was cleared and ready for farming, Papa grew all kinds of row crops (vegetables that were sold roadside and at the farmers' market) and raised a variety of farm animals.

In order to build his house, he had to cut logs and then have them sawed at the sawmill into lumber. With this lumber, Papa built a four-room house. This was some good lumber because the house stood for almost a hundred years. The wood was kept natural and was never painted. Papa lived and raised his family in this house until 1930, when he built a new house. There was no electricity in this old house, as it was heated by a fireplace, and lights were provided by kerosene lamps. The food was cooked over the fireplace in the living room, or on a woodstove located on the back porch. All the food they had was raised on the farm or harvested from the woods and river. This house only had two beds, and all of the children slept in the same bedroom. Dad said when a big blowing snow happened that it sometimes blew the snow through the cracks and you could shake the snow off the covers in the morning when you woke up. This old house, built in 1917, stood until 2011 when the April 27 tornado blew the top off. The original tin roof was still on the house up until this time. The scrap metal off the old house brought three hundred dollars, which is what Papa had paid for the entire farm ninety-four years ago.

Papa and Granny Woodard raised nine children, and my father was the third child. When my father and mother were married, my dad had to immediately go to

World War II where he served four years in the Pacific. His company made seven landings and successfully took seven islands. Their company spent four weeks training for their next assignment, which would have been a landing on the main island of Japan. The war ended with the dropping of the atomic bombs, saving them from having to invade mainland Japan.

Everyone was proud when my dad returned home alive because he had a lot of narrow escapes during his service. He was an antiaircraft gunner, shooting down enemy planes while both on ships and on land. Many of these planes were Kamikaze planes headed straight for their ship. He was given a hero's welcome upon his return by our community, and everyone was proud of his service to our country.

During the war, my mother stayed with the Woodard family, working on the farm and living in the house with Papa and Granny Woodard with all of their children that were still left at home. Granny Woodard taught my mother many things about cooking and sewing. Papa had built a new house a few years earlier before the Great Depression. When my dad returned from the war, he and my mother lived in Papa's old house for a short time. It was the same as described earlier, just older. This was where my brother was born. My brother remembers Mom telling him about the night he was born in the old house while snow was blowing in through the cracks. People did not go to the hospital to have their babies back then. If the midwife that helped deliver the baby needed a doctor, one would be sent for and brought to the house. The night my brother was born, a doctor was indeed needed. So Dr. Brown made the trip in the snow to come out and deliver my brother.

My dad, mother, and brother lived in the old house until my father could build a new house. Dad started building the new house in 1949, and it was unfinished in 1950 when my dad, mother, and brother moved in. This new house was the house I was raised up in. Before I was born, the doctor had advised my mother to go to the hospital. So I was born in the Gordon and Patton Hospital in Oneonta, Alabama, in 1951.

Our new house was also a four-room house. The house had a kitchen, living room, two bedrooms, and a nice front porch. It had a woodstove, a table and cane bottom chairs for the kitchen, a couch and chairs for the living room, a full bed with a dresser and mirror for my parents' bedroom, and two half beds and some drawers to put clothes in for my brother and me. It did not take much money to maintain this house because it was heated by a fireplace, and we cut all the wood to burn in the fireplace with a crosscut saw and ax. We did not have a phone, television, air-conditioner, bathrooms, or running water in the house. We did have electricity in the house for five light bulbs (one for each room and the porch). Having electricity was a big improvement over the old house that my parents first started housekeeping in.

When I was about six years old, my mother got a new electric stove and a wringer washing machine. She was very happy to get the new appliances. I remember when Mother got the new electric stove. Even with the new stove, we still kept the old woodstove in the house for heating water and the occasional cooking and canning of food to save on the electric bill. I remember that Mother always kept a kettle of water on the woodstove, since we did not have a hot water heater or running water in the house at this time. The woodstove also provided the house with heat in the winter. It was mine and my brother's job to keep wood on the porch for the fireplace and the woodstove.

The new wringer washer, which we kept on our front porch, changed the way Mother washed clothes. She would no longer have to wash them in a number three washtub on a rub board. After washing, she would put the clothes on the line outside to dry. I remember one day when I was helping my mother wash clothes, I accidentally stuck my hand in the rollers, and it pulled my arm in. With some quick thinking, my mother unplugged the power cord to stop the washing machine, and I was able to get my arm out. Luckily, it was not broken, and I was fine. It just scared Mother to death when she first saw my arm caught between the rollers but was relieved once she knew that I was okay.

In the old house, light was from a kerosene lamp, and cooking was done over the fireplace or woodstove. Although having electricity in the new house was a big improvement, my dad would not let us burn a light bulb unless you absolutely needed it. If you were not reading or working on something, all the lights had better be off, and we would only burn a kerosene lamp.

Sometimes, we would even just go out and sit on the front porch at night with only the moon and stars for light. One thing was for sure, you better not leave a light on in a room and not be in there; Dad did not allow this.

One thing that stands out in my memory about our house while growing up was the floor. We did not have a finished floor; only a subfloor made of sawmill-cut lumber. Since it was put down green, as it dried, it left big cracks in the floor. I knew I had better not drop a penny or something small on the floor because it would fall through the cracks in the floor. If I did, I would have to crawl up under the house to try to find whatever was dropped. I crawled under the house on several occasions to find stuff that we lost through the floor.

Years later, Dad covered the living room with a finished hardwood floor, and Mother picked out some nice rugs to cover the kitchen and bedrooms. When we got the new floors, we sure thought they were nice. The walls were rough-cut boards with only shingles covering them on the outside to protect them from the weather. The house had no insulation, so it would get very cold in the winter. When the wind was blowing hard, I could feel the cold air coming through the walls.

We had to draw all of our water for cooking, drinking, and bathing from the well with a bucket. Mother washed all of the dishes and vegetables in dishpans in water that we brought from the well several times a day. Mother would heat water for baths in dishpans on the woodstove until she got an electric stove. I still remember the bath order. Mother was first, then Dad in the same water, and then clean water for my brother and me—and I luckily got to go first. Then out with the dirty water. All of our bathing was done in a number three washtub in the kitchen.

My chores were putting firewood on the porch, shelling corn, and feeding the chickens, hogs, horses, and mules. In addition, lots of work raising cotton, corn, and all kinds of vegetables. When we finished our chores at home, it was off to Papa and Granny's house to help them with their chores. These were basically a repeat of ours, except Papa always wanted things done his way.

Mother and Dad would usually take care of milking the cow. As I got older, I did do some of the milking, but Mother was always very particular and clean with the milk, so most of the time, she and Dad handled that chore. We did not have a refrigerator, so we stored our milk in the spring or well to keep it cool. We did not really need a refrigerator because all of our food was fresh from the fields in the summer and from stored or canned food in a jar for the winter. Mother had put up all this canned food in the summer so that we would have it during the winter. Later on, we got an icebox that you put a chunk of ice in, and it would keep things cool for days. Mother would take the bucket of milk and pour it twice through a cloth strainer to remove the cream from the milk. Mother would put that cream in a churn, along with some milk, and make butter out of it. She would set the churns on the hearth by the fireplace. Mother could make some really good butter to go on her homemade biscuits. Breakfast was really delicious, made with eggs gathered from the henhouse, bacon from the hog we killed, and homemade biscuits from the woodstove, served with a fresh glass of raw cow's milk. I have always said homemade biscuits made from a woodstove were the best biscuits you could eat. Mother was especially good at cooking, and homemade biscuits were one of her specialities.

Mother was afraid to let the fire burn in the fireplace at night. We would bank it up with the coals that were left from the wood after the fire had burned out. It would get very cold at night. I would sleep with my head covered up, with only my nose stuck out from under the covers. I would wake up in the morning with my nose really cold. It was the exact opposite in the summer; we would get very hot. We slept with the windows up, our pillows in the windowsills, and our heads practically out the window to keep cool. It would usually be about ten o'clock at night before the house would cool down. It must have been healthy because we rarely got sick.

During the winter, I remember we had plenty of covers because Mother always had a quilt up on the quilting frames in the living room. She was very good at quilting, making many beautiful quilts throughout her lifetime. She also crocheted, sewed, knitted, and made everything that we needed for our home.

One of the chores that my brother and I had was gathering up kindling to start fires in the early morning. Dad would get up and use this kindling to have the fire going good by breakfast. I remember how good it was to back up to the fireplace in the early mornings to warm up. Mornings started early at our house. Dad would hit the wall one time and say, "Get up!" And when you heard that hit on the wall, you had better be at the table, ready to eat in just a few minutes. Dad would not tell you twice, and there was certainly no such thing as going back to bed. He believed that everyone should get up and eat breakfast at the same time together because that was how he was raised. In our house, breakfast was the most important meal of the day. After breakfast, there was a list of things to do, and then we were off to work or school.

It was an exciting day when Dad put in an electric well pump. This gave Mother running water and a sink in the house. This excited us so much, and in the summer, we could spray each other with the water hose to cool off after a hard day's work. It was also a great way to take a bath, and to stay out of the number three washtub.

When I was seven or eight, we got our first refrigerator. Shortly after that, we got a radio, and Mother got an electric mixer. We had so much stuff running on electricity that Dad was beginning to complain about the three-dollar electric bill. Mother also learned how to drive during this time. Dad let her practice in the old log truck, and then she got her driver's license, driving a 1955 Ford pickup truck with a crack in its windshield. One day while Papa was driving down a hill, hauling a bale of cotton in the truck bed, he hit the brakes hard while I was standing up in the seat. There was no such thing as seat belts in those days, and I flew into the windshield head first, causing the windshield to crack. After that, for a long time, they said I was a hardheaded boy. My wife says I still am.

When I was sixteen, my dad bought a new house that had been built only two years before. It had cold and hot running water—and even a telephone! It had inside bathrooms with a shower and tub, three bedrooms, a large living room, and a modern kitchen that my mother loved. The house was warm and insulated and gave us all a new style of life. In this house, we worked and bought our first television. I actually saw my first movie that year. We had all the conveniences of modern living, except for an air-conditioner. Most houses in the 1960s did not have air-conditioners. After all the years of going to the bathroom outside in the woods, it sure was hard getting used to going inside. It was nice to see Mother have all the conveniences in the kitchen to cook our meals. Dad was still saying the electric bill was too high and to "Cut the lights off!" Life really changed in those sixteen years. We started to buy our milk and butter from the store, and for the first time, our grocery bill was over ten dollars a week.

My father was a conservative man, especially when it came to money. So he had a plan to save on that grocery bill. He planted enough potatoes so that we could furnish Piggly Wiggly (a local grocery store) 100 ten pound bags of potatoes each week. We would plow potatoes up every Thursday and have them washed and bagged by Friday so they could be delivered when he carried Mother to the grocery store. They got groceries and had money left over from the sale of the potatoes. Even though he tried to be very conservative with money, he was proud to get Mother all the things that she needed or wanted. He taught us to work and save and that carried us a long way in our life.

When I Thought
I Was a Cowboy

When I was young, I could not wait to get my own horse. I was always around big horses and mules, but I wanted to have my very own horse that I could call my own. When I was around eleven, my dad bought a solid white pony for my Christmas present. I had a lot of fun riding this little pony. At this time in my life, I felt like a real cowboy. I rode this pony for several years. This was a great experience as a child that I will always remember. I learned a lot of the basic skills about riding which prepared me to ride later. We never had a saddle, so we always rode bareback. We had a big white horse called Dan that we could ride, but he was so big I needed help to get on his back. We could not ride him unless my dad or my granddad was there to get him out and stay with us while we rode. When we rode Dan, we could only let him walk. Dad wanted to take good care of him because he was very valuable to our family. He was part-Belgian and part-Morgan. We used him for all kinds of work, but we mainly used him to plow. Dan also had to snake logs and pull stumps out of the ground. We had a big sled that Dan would pull. We would fill the sled with corn and firewood, and Dan would pull it to where it needed to go. It was lots of fun to ride on the sled pulled by Dan. But when I got up on Dan's back, as a young boy, I really felt like a cowboy.

Finally, around fourteen years of age, I bought my first quarter horse. I called him Red, but I should have called him Flash because this horse could really run. I rode this horse bareback. I taught him to neck-rein. I could ride this horse without a bridle because I could guide the horse with my feet and stop him with a pull on the mane and the command *whoa*. I also taught this horse to jump poles about three feet high. I would race my friends on this horse, and he would always win. We had lots of fun riding Red. Most of my friends had a horse, and we would go riding on Sunday afternoon, sometimes all the way to Austin Creek. We would be gone all afternoon. We began to think we were real cowboys.

Our neighbor would buy horses from the sale and get all the boys in the community to come and break them on Sunday afternoon. We spent more time in the plowed-up dirt after being thrown off than we did on the horses' backs, but the number of boys riding would finally wear them down, and we would soon have them broken to ride. When we broke a horse to ride, my neighbor would sell it and would have another one for us the next Sunday afternoon. On these occasions, we really thought we were cowboys.

On one occasion, we all rode our horses for trick-or-treating. This was one night that always stood out in my mind, not so much for riding the horses but for what we received from the neighbors. We rode our horses from house to house. On the first stop, we received a couple of baked sweet potatoes, the next house a banana, the next some peanuts, and then an apple. As we continued from house to house, we got a lot of the same stuff, but that was what people had to give back in those days, and that was what every child received when they went trick-or-treating. We rode all the way through the community and did not get one piece of candy. We did not have time to go to many houses because everyone went to bed early in those days. We also had to go in and visit with all the neighbors to get our treat. We did enjoy the visits with everyone. We were very appreciative and proud of what we received on that Halloween night. It is one of my best memories of how simple life was back then. Riding the horses that night was one night to remember, and also, it was a lot better than walking.

I finally got so comfortable riding Red that one day, I thought I would rope a calf off my horse like a rodeo rider. I practiced with my rope and thought I was good with the lasso. I was good enough to get the rope over the calf's head the first try. That was when all the excitement began. I was riding bareback, and that was my first mistake because that calf pulled me off that horse in a blink of an eye. I hit the ground belly first holding on to that rope because I wanted to rope him, and the calf dragged me several feet before I was able to get up on my feet. I had caught a calf, and I was not about to let go of that rope. The calf was headed to the woods, and I was running along behind him, trying to pull on the rope enough to slow him down. Suddenly, I saw a plan right in front of me: a tree. I ran toward the tree as fast as I could and wrapped the rope around the tree just in time because when the calf got to the end of his rope, it turned him a flip, and the calf hit the ground. I had caught a calf, but it was the hard way! At this point in my life, I felt that I was a cowboy, but at my age today, I see now that I just thought I was a cowboy.

On another occasion when I thought I was a cowboy was on a day when my dad and I were hauling some bull calves to the sale on the pickup truck with wooden sideboards. As we loaded the calves, one calf got his head between the sideboards and the tailgate of the truck. That was all it took for him to break out. I did not have any time to think, so my response was to jump around the calf's head and throw him to the ground like the cowboys bulldogging calves did at the rodeo. I had actually done this several times before, successfully. We would sometimes throw the calves on the ground to give them a worm pill with a bolus gun. But throwing this calf to the ground would be one I would remember. After four or five bounces across the field, I finally twisted his head and threw the calf on the ground. I went down to the ground on the calf's head to pin him, but the calf thrust his head upward into my ribs—breaking two of my ribs. I could not breathe deep for a month and still have two knots on my ribs today as the results of this injury. This was another day of being a cowboy! But as I see it today that was another time in my life in which I just thought I was a cowboy.

The last attempt of trying to be a cowboy was when I was old enough to know better. But being older and knowing better usually never stopped me. I lassoed a cow off the tractor and jumped off onto the ground to try to hold it till my son could get back to help me. I was holding the cow, and it was going around and around. Every time the cow went around, the long end of the rope on the ground was wrapping around my right leg. All of a sudden, the cow broke out in a straight run, jerking my legs right out from under me in a blink of an eye. The cow was now pulling me across the pasture on my back because my leg was hung in the rope. I began to roll to get the rope free from my leg, and after a short pull on the ground, I was able to free my leg. Thank goodness I got loose. It could have been a lot worse, but it taught me a valuable lesson to not ever try that again. I remembered from that day that you learn by doing.

All these valuable learning experiences of working with animals and tying to be a cowboy were a lot of fun in my early days, especially riding the horses. I had some other learning experiences like the day a bull stepped on my foot and sent me to the emergency room because I was too close to him. Another day, a bull called 878 was in a catch chute, and we were going to put a tag in his ear, but he sent me to the emergency room instead, with me thinking that my hand was broken. Unbelievably, it was not broken. Another day, a cow kicked me in the back of the leg, turning it blue from my hip to my ankle. A bull kicked a gate back into my head, causing a big knot on my head right between the eyes. What was funny about that was when I got the bull to the vet, he asked,

"And which do I need to doctor first, you or the bull?" All of these encounters and near misses turned out okay, just some injuries, but as I think back on those days, one thing comes to mind that it all occurred on days when I thought I was a cowboy.

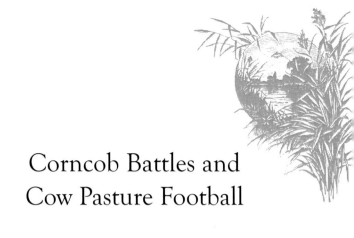

Corncob Battles and
Cow Pasture Football

By the time we reached our teenage years, we all thought we were tough boys. This was probably due to the types of games we played as we were growing up. You do not forget being tackled in a fresh pile of cow manure! Boys today do not play these types of games, and I do not recommend that they do so. That was a different time back then, and no one was thinking about getting hurt or hurting anybody. We were just having fun playing as boys played back then.

I wrestled and played king of the mountain as far back as I can remember. Usually, wrestling was with a group of boys, and it was simple: you won the game if you were the last man standing. We also had our one-on-one wrestling matches, which were usually concluded when someone would yell, "calf rope." That meant you were pinned, or usually, when you were hurting bad enough that you yelled, "calf rope", and then the match was over.

I was very good at wrestling because I was so quick and was rarely ever pinned. I did love to wrestle and even took wrestling when I attended Auburn University, majoring in physical education, and I made a very good grade and was top in my wrestling class. Maybe the wrestling skills I acquired during my growing up years helped me in this class.

King of the mountain was also a fun game. We would find a big embankment or hill, and one person started at the top as the king. It was everyone's goal to climb up the embankment and take over the king position at the top by throwing the man at the top off. Then you would become the king of the mountain. The most fun was rolling back down the embankment after someone threw you off. I would have to say this type of game made us tough and strong. We had a lot of fun playing it. It also made us have endurance because we played it for hours at a time.

Another game was putting someone in an old tractor tire and rolling them down the hill. This was very dangerous because my cousin broke his collar bone one day when he was going so fast that he was thrown out of the tire.

Every spring when the fresh ground was plowed, we had dirt clod battle games. This game was to simply see if you could take the dirt clods and hit someone at thirty or forty yards away. We would lie down in the dirt and hide behind terrace rows in the field to try to get out of the line of fire from the oncoming clods. We would pop up and try to throw one before getting hit. This came to a very quick halt one day when I accidently threw a dirt clod with a rock inside. I did not know there was a rock inside. This clod hit my best friend right above his eye, resulting into a deep cut, and he had to go to the doctor to get stitches. His mom only said that boys would be boys. I felt really bad about hurting him.

Usually, all these games were played on Sunday afternoon after church because every boy would meet at somebody's house for a corncob battle or a Sunday afternoon game of football in the cow pasture. Commonly called "cow pasture ball"; this was a simple game of tackle football without the pads. We played in the cow pasture because this was the only place that had grass to fall on and had enough space. Mostly, everyone's yard back then was dirt. The fields were all planted in corn, cotton, or some other row crop, so the only place we had to play football was in somebody's cow pasture. The corncob battles were either every man for himself, or we would pick teams. No rules applied in this game.

I remembered my neighbor invited his cousin from the city to come visit one Sunday afternoon. He had never been in a corncob battle. He tried his first corncob battle with the country boys that afternoon, and boy, was he in for a shock when he got hit right between the eyes in the first few minutes of the battle! It was an awakening for him! He told me years later he was not expecting anything like that. If you got tired or hurt, you just simply ran away to the yard and stopped playing the game. But usually, everyone had so much honor and pride that no one would quit and give up even if you got a knot on the head. We would throw these corn cobs at each other with the intention of making it hurt. The dry corn cobs would sting, but if you got hit by one that someone had picked up out of a cow patty that was wet with manure, it would really hurt you—plus you got cow patty mess all over you. This, most of the time, came with a laugh and the saying, "Boy, I got you!" It's a wonder that we did not get hurt playing this game because we were running all around in the barn, jumping out of barn lofts and jumping over fences, and of course, we would hide behind anything to keep from getting hit like a bale of hay, or even a cow or horse. Sometimes, we would grab a friend and hide behind him. You really got the advantage if you got control of the corn crib, where all the corn cobs were located and the corn had been shelled. All I can remember after this game is we had a few red places and a few small knots from being hit by these flying corn cobs and a few splatters of cow manure on us.

This game was really safe compared to the game of cow pasture football. We met at someone's house almost every Sunday afternoon for a game of football. Everyone was tough and brave, but no one was brave enough to say, "Let's play tag football" because if you did, you would be laughed at and made fun of. It was understood if you played football, it was going to be full tackle without the pads on, and you were probably going to be tackled in a pile of fresh cow manure before the game was over. It was always a big laugh when someone was tackled and splattered in a fresh pile of cow poop. Before you played in this game, you needed to be big and strong or be able to run fast. I was lucky that I could outrun everybody. I did get tackled sometimes, took some hard licks, and landed in some cow patties in these games that I still remember today. It made us all tough because I don't ever remember anyone getting seriously injured like with a blown-out knee or a broken arm. I assure you we all had strong ligaments and strong bones from the raw cow's milk and food we had back in those days. I really enjoyed these games we had on Sunday afternoons and felt it made me a better football player when I started playing quarterback on the high school's football team.

We started playing these types of games at an early age, which conditioned our bodies, for it is one of the reasons I think we did not get many serious injuries. I am not sure today's young people could go back to this kind of play because their bodies have not been conditioned to this type of rigorous play from a very young age. It was a different time that will never be returned to. But I did enjoy those memories of these types of fun games that we created for ourselves. But I certainly do not recommend any young people to play these games. If you do, then wear a helmet, eye goggles, and certainly, wear proper pads for tackle football for your safety. Also, you might want to play on a football field so you will not have the memories of falling down and hitting a fresh cow manure pile!

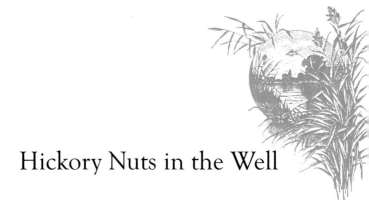

Hickory Nuts in the Well

Most of the time, we had chores to do when we were growing up on the farm. Chores like shucking and shelling the corn, feeding the chickens and hogs, putting firewood on the porch, and many other jobs. We were in the field most of the time working, but occasionally, we would have some playtime. We would ride our bicycles, play softball, make mud pies, and build small fish ponds in the yard for fun. We loved going barefooted and playing in the mud and water, and this usually kept us entertained. I was only about five or six years of age, and my brother was ten or eleven at this time.

One day playing out in the yard, we found some new excitement we could not resist. My older brother and cousin found that dropping hickory nuts in the well made a splashing sound and echoed up the pipe in the well. We were intrigued by the new sounds of echoes in the well pipes. We all liked hearing the hickory nuts hit in the bottom of the well, making this splashing sound. So we all started gathering hickory nuts up out of the yard to put in the well. At first, we could hear a splashing sound, but after dropping several nuts in the well, it quickly turned to a clicking sound when the nuts hit the bottom. The hickory nuts were floating on the surface and are now just piling up on top of each other. I think we put about every hickory nut we found in the yard into the well. That was a good many, since we had two large hickory nut trees in the yard.

This was a drilled well that we got all of our water from to do all the drinking, cooking, washing, and taking baths. We did not have running water in the house as people do today. Every drop of our water used in the house had to be pulled up from the well by hands turning the windlass handle and drawing it up in a well bucket. This well had a well bucket that was long and slender. We tied a rope to the bucket to let it down in the well. The rope that held the bucket was tied to a well windlass. You would let the bucket down in the well using the windlass system. The windlass had a handle to turn the rope around a round piece of wood with a steel rod through it. By turning the handle, you could pull the bucket of water back to the top full of water. Even though this was hard, it was easier than just pulling it up just by your hands. There was a release handle at the top to pull to let the water out of the long well bucket into another water bucket that could be carried into the house.

Now, with the well filled several feet with floating hickory nuts, it would be impossible to get the well bucket through the hickory nuts to the water. We did not think of this as we were filling the well full of hickory nuts. It was so much fun we didn't think about not having any water. When mother found out about the well being full of hickory nuts, she said, "You children will be in trouble when your daddy gets home from work." Sure enough, when Dad got home and found out he could not get water from the well because it was full of hickory nuts, he was not happy. When he got through with us, we never did want to put another hickory nut in a well again. He tried for days to get them out, but I don't think he ever got all them out. To get our water while he was working on the well, we had to haul it from my papa Woodard's spring, which was a quarter mile away. I can really understand now why he was so upset with us. It was one day that we all remember in the memories of growing up on the farm. I guess we were just being normal children growing up and learning our lessons. But no one ever had to tell us not to put hickory nuts in the well again.

Games We Played

We had plenty of work to do on the farm but always had time to play games in the late afternoon and Sundays. Games like marbles, horseshoes, mumble peg, and checkers were some of the milder type games we played. One of the extreme games we played was riding and trying to stay on a flying jenny.

The game of marbles was as simple as putting ten of your marbles in the center of a ring drawn on the ground that was about three feet in diameter. You needed ground that had a smooth surface. If four people played this game, you would have forty marbles in the ring. To see who would shoot first, we would draw a line on the ground, and at a set distance, we would shoot our marble toward the line, and whoever got closest to the line would get the first shot. Sometimes, we would just pull straws to determine who would go first. I always liked shooting for the line because I was good at that. The pulling of straws was by luck only. All the marbles were placed in the center of the ring. The first person shooting would have to shoot from outside the line of the circle. If you knocked the marble out of the circle, then you got another shot. You could continue shooting until the shooter marble went outside the circle, or the marble that you were shooting at did not go outside circle. Wherever your shooter marble landed inside the circle was where you had to shoot from. A person would shoot the marble by thumping with his thumb a marble placed between his finger and thumb. If the marble the person was shooting at did not go out of the circle or the shooter marble went outside the circle, then it was the next person's turn.

Most of the time, we played for fun, and everyone after the game walked away with their ten marbles. If you played for "keeps", you walked away with the ones you knocked out of the ring. I sometimes cleaned the ring full of marbles and never missed knocking a marble out of the ring on every shot, not even allowing anyone else a shot. We played marbles at school every day at lunch. If you got caught playing for "keeps", you would get a paddling. After we finished our lunch, we could go outside to the circle and play marbles or smear football. I found it more profitable playing marbles, but I played both.

Horseshoes was a game everyone played. Every family had horseshoes and two stakes put up in the yard for playing this game. Horseshoes was an all-American game involving children and adults. It was fun to throw a horseshoe toward the stake and ring the stake, or to throw and lean a horseshoe up against the stake and score points. Horseshoes was the only game I knew that you could get points for just getting close. That was where the saying came from that says "Getting close only counts in horseshoes."

Mumble peg was a game we played by throwing and flipping a knife to see if we could make the knife stick up in the ground. Before the game began, we drove a stick into the ground with our pocketknife, and the loser of the game had to pull this stick up out of the ground with his teeth. We would flip a pocketknife off of fingers, arms, knees, shoulders, head, etc. to see if the knife would stick into the ground. We also loved throwing knifes into trees and targets to see who had the best knife-throwing skill.

I have sat and played many hours behind a checkerboard. My family enjoyed this game for many generations. My grandpa, my dad, myself, and my son and daughter have all played and enjoyed playing checkers. We enjoyed many hours of playing this game at our house and at my grandpa's house. My son always loved to play this game as a young boy with his grandfather and his older relatives—just as I did as a young boy.

One of the most extreme games we played was riding a flying jenny. My uncle made one of these for us when we were children to ride. A flying jenny was made by cutting down a tree and leaving the stump three or four feet high from the ground. You would find a long 2x8 board as long as you could find, usually about twenty feet long. You would then put a big bolt through the center of the twenty foot board and place the bolt in a drilled hole in the center of the stump with washers placed between the board and the stump. You would turn the bolt down into the hole until the bolt became very tight. Then, you put plenty of oil or grease on the bolt and the hole in the board so the board would spin on the bolt and on top of the stump. A person would push it around and around usually from inside close to the stump. That person would have to be careful not to get hit by the board. Two people would ride with one sitting on each end of the 2x8 board. The 2x4 boards were nailed onto the 2x8 so you could hang on as the board went around and around on the stump. If someone pushed it very fast you would eventually get to going so fast you would occasionally get slung off. It did not feel good when you hit the ground. If you did manage to stay on for any length of time it would make you very dizzy. It was a wonder that some of us did not get killed on this flying jenny because it was so dangerous to ride but it was even more dangerous to push! We had a lot of fun riding it because it was a little scary and because of the height and speed. When you got thrown off it would hurt some but it was like riding a horse, you would get right back on. You had to be careful if you were doing the pushing because if you didn't watch carefully it could come around and hit you in the head. I do not advise anyone to try this because it is very dangerous. Thank God he was with us on this extreme activity keeping us safe.

The Christmas Day Splash

One of my adventures occurred on a cold Christmas day. I had a chance to head for my friend's house, knowing he was going to visit his grandma. This meant eating some very good home cooking, drinking fresh cow's milk, and eating the best chocolate cake ever made. It also meant adventure on a creek near his grandma's house.

After dinner on that Christmas day, we were ready to go outside for some adventure. My friend's grandma said, "Ya'll don't get out of the yard." We thought that meant "don't get off the one-hundred acre farm." So down to the barn we go, on out to the fields to look for arrowheads, and then straight on down to the creek for some fun and adventures. We are now "out of the yard," and we kindly know it. We cannot wait to see what adventures are ahead, so up the creek we go.

We had watched television at his house, just enough to see some Tarzan movies. That was one of the first shows I remember seeing on our neighbors' television. It looked like he was having fun swinging on vines from tree to tree. So we thought we could do that. We had those types of vines in the woods. It did not take us long to find a good Tarzan vine in our woods. We could not swing from tree to tree, but some of the vines we could swing out very far and high and back to the same spot you left from. We found some vines in tall trees in deep hollows that you could swing on all the way across the hollow and land on the other side. We played on these vines every chance we got.

Going up that creek that Christmas day was lots of fun. It did not take us long to travel up the creek to find what we thought was the perfect Tarzan vine. It was in a very tall tree right on the edge of the creek bank. The vine was hanging from a limb that was extending way out over the water. We always had our knife, so we cut the vine off at the bottom and next to the ground. We were so excited we had the perfect vine to swing on. It appeared this was one of best vines we had ever found. We could swing out several feet and very high. We were having lots of fun swinging out over the water and back to the bank. Then the thought came to me that I just might be able to swing all the way across the creek and land on the other side.

I took the first attempt. I took a running go and jumped off the creek bank about five feet above the water. My feet left the ground, and I swung way out high over the creek. However, I saw that I could not make it to the other side because the farther out I swung, the higher I went. I did not make it to the other side on this attempt, but I planned to try again. I was determined to jump from the vine in midair and land on the other side—for no other reason except that I wanted to see if I could.

However, all good things must come to an end. I got a good run and a strong push from the bank, swinging farther and higher than before, but the vine broke when I was at the highest point. It seemed like things paused for a second, and then I went down and hit the cold, frigid waters, making a big splash on that cold Christmas day. I swam to the bank in freezing cold water. My clothes were soaking wet.

Wait a minute; we were not supposed to be "out of the yard." What were we going to do? We did not want to get in trouble, so I can't go up to the house soaking wet. We put our minds together and came up with a plan. We knew that my friend's grandma always kept matches in the kitchen to light the woodstove. So my friend would go to the house and go into the kitchen like he was getting us something to eat, but also pick up some matches to build us a fire to dry my clothes. He was successful on his mission and was back with the food and the matches shortly.

We built a fire then put a pole over the fire to hang the clothes on. Yes, I stripped them off and put them on the pole to dry. It was very cold on that Christmas day. The fire felt very good, and it was also drying my clothes. The fire began to die down, so we finished putting it out, and I put my clothes back on. Mission accomplished. My clothes were now dry. It all seemed like the plan had worked. We might not get in trouble after all. Wait a minute, my clothes smelled like smoke. I won't be able to go into the house because someone would smell the smoke on my clothes. When we get ourselves "back in the yard," I roll in the dirt to try to kill the smoke smell on my clothes, and I also stay outside. I have dirt from head to toe. The plan must have worked because when my friend's parents picked us up, nothing was said about the smoke smell. They said, "Did ya'll have fun?" We said, "We sure did!" I hardly said another word all the way home. I was hoping that mother would not smell the smoke when I got home. When I got home, mother did not ask me about the smoke smell on my clothes, so the dirt trick saved the day!

Years later, I was telling the story to my mother about falling in the creek on that Christmas day. All she said was "God was looking out for ya'll on that day." This was one day that I will never forget, the day the Tarzan vine broke, and I made a big splash into the creek on that cold Christmas day.

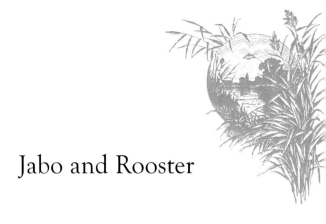

Jabo and Rooster

Jabo was my first beagle dog that I owned. He was just a puppy when I got him. He was given to me by Mr. Blackwood, a neighbor that had some good beagles known for running rabbits. It was not long before Jabo was running rabbits. Jabo was lazy by nature. It may have been because he did not have a mate. He would always lie on the back doorsteps or out under a shade tree and wait until I headed for the woods, then he would get up and head out to find a rabbit to run. Most of the time, Jabo would wait for me to jump a rabbit for him. Jabo would run the trail with his nose right on the ground. He could not run fast, so he never could catch any rabbits. The rabbit would run in a few circles and cross his tracks leaving a scent trail for Jabo. Jabo would run that trail all evening, while the rabbit was hiding over in the next thicket—probably laughing at him. The rabbit we jumped most of the time was the same rabbit. But Jabo would chase him every day anyway because he did not know the difference. I believe the rabbit enjoyed the chase as much as we did. I only had this one dog, and he

Robert Earl Woodard

was in need of a friend or a mate. It was very unusual how Jabo would find his friend.

One day, a chicken truck was going up the road with a big load of chickens. These chickens were locked up in chicken coups. One of the white roosters was able to escape through a small hole in the coup. While jumping from the truck, the rooster hurt one of his wings. I found the rooster beside the road with a severe injury. He probably broke the wing because when I found him, the wing was hanging down with blood on it. I picked him up and carried him to the house. We had plenty of chickens at the barn, so one more would not be a problem. However, I could not take an injured chicken to the barn. He would not have a good chance of living because the other chickens would peck him and not accept an injured rooster. Also, the other roosters at the barn would try to hurt him. We needed to keep him in the house, but I knew that was not going to happen because we had already nursed a wounded owl back to health inside the house several months earlier. After the owl's wing healed, he flew out of the big box we kept him in. The reason this was a big problem was that I had talked mother into keeping the owl in the house to doctor him. I told mother I would keep the owl in a big box by the wood heater. One day after the owl had recovered, he escaped from his box and was flying all over the place in the house. In all the excitement of trying to catch the owl, he pooped on Mother's clean floor. Mother said, "This owl has got to go and no more animals can come in the house." We released the owl the next day to fly away.

After that experience, there would be no need to ask mother to bring a chicken into the house to doctor it back to health. The next best thing would be to put him in a box under the back doorsteps. Mother normally did not allow chickens to be in the yard, but she said okay this time. If the chickens from the barn got in the yard, she would chase them out of the yard with a broom, or put Jabo after them and he would chase them out. After asking mother, she did allow me to put the chicken outside under the back doorsteps. After a while of feeding the chicken in the box, he recovered and became a pet. All this time, the chicken was under the doorstep while Jabo was laying on top of the doorsteps. We did not know that these two animals would become best friends. Jabo was definitely the leader. Wherever Jabo went, the chicken we now called Rooster would follow. If Jabo would lie down on the back steps, then Rooster would get as close to him as he could. I remember seeing Jabo and Rooster lying side by side, touching each other in the yard. I remember seeing Jabo running across the yard and seeing Rooster chase in behind him. Jabo didn't follow Rooster; it was always Rooster chasing in behind Jabo. Rooster did not have to eat with the chickens at the barn because we fed him and Jabo at the back door together. This rooster ate so much that he got very fat and waddled when he walked. Mother always threw scraps out for him and Jabo, and I watched them eat out of the same pan. It did not only amaze me but amazed the entire family how Jabo and Rooster got along and formed the bond of being best friends. Now, Jabo had himself a friend, but Jabo never taught Rooter how to run rabbits. The fun they had together was playing in the yard and being friends.

The Cotton-Picking Contest

My father always challenged us to do our best. He would accomplish this by example, outworking all of us and working harder than anyone in the community. He would challenge us every day by telling us what tasks we had to complete by the end of the day. He would also tell us if we finished the job, we could have some fun after the job was completed. Most of the time, the reward would be to go to the river to fish or swim, or to the woods to hunt or just explore.

I always found it hard to outdo him because he seemed like Superman. Not only did he farm during the day, but he also welded tanks in Birmingham until one o'clock at night. He was always up the next morning at six o'clock—getting us up for school or getting us up for the job we had to do on that day.

In the fall of 1963, we made some really good cotton. I was only twelve years old, but at this age, I could already pick over 200 pounds per day. Mother could pick 250 pounds and fix dinner, but Dad could get 300 pounds every day.

One pretty fall day, Dad somehow got me to tell him I would beat him picking cotton. I challenged him knowing I would have to break my record and get over 300 pounds to beat him. We left the house at six o'clock and were picking cotton by six fifteen. I started picking as fast as I could, taking a row and a half. When I got my sack full, I did not go weigh it. I just got another sack and continued picking. At eleven fifteen, it was time to weigh up our cotton. I weighed up at 176 pounds. Dad said he had 175, although he may have been playing games with me, letting me think I was winning and he was close behind. I did not take long for lunch, as there was no rule on when you could start back. I knew I would start back before my dad so I could get a head start. The work that evening was very hard. My fingers were getting very sore from all the burs that would stick my fingers, and my back was very tired from bending over and from pulling the pick sack all day. I was determined to win the contest, so I pushed on, pulling that heavy sack and putting all the cotton in that sack as fast as I could. At four o'clock that afternoon, Dad announced it was time to weigh up all the cotton. Dad weighed my cotton first, and I had broken my record: my total for the day was 301 pounds!

Now, it was time to see if I had beaten my dad. He weighed his cotton and said he had 300 pounds. Then he told me that I had won the contest. I knew we had some daylight left, and we had never stopped that early in the day. However, on that day, he told me to get my pick sack and go rest on it under the shade because I had won. I sure was glad he did because I was so tired I could not move. After calling the contest over, Dad went back to picking cotton. He picked another 60 pounds before dark. Dad had declared me the winner—and that was all that mattered to me at the time.

I do remember that day in my life very clearly, but I remember that night even more because I was so tired I could not sleep. I was hurting so badly from working so hard and fast I thought I was going to die. I know my dad picked more cotton than I did on that day, but he sure made me feel good about winning the contest. After that day, it was not hard for Mother, Dad and me to pick 1400 pounds in two days. You needed 1400 pounds to make a 500-pound bale after it had been ginned.

There are some days in your life you just don't forget. That was one of those days. I will never forget the day my dad said I had won the cotton-picking contest.

A Bicycle Saved My Life

On several occasions, I broke my record running the one-hundred yard dash. However, on one occasion, I broke my record riding my bicycle faster than ever, which ended up saving my life.

I was ten or eleven years of age and had just been riding a bicycle for a couple of years. This was before Highway 79 was paved, and it was still a dirt road. The state was building the new Highway 79 and had the base built of dirt. This made it very dusty, so not many cars would take this road, and if they did travel it, they would go very slow. Most cars would travel Highway 231, which was paved and was the road in front of my house. Highway 79 was being built at the back of our house about three hundred yards away. There was a dirt road beside our house that went between the two highways. This was where I would ride my bike.

It was a normal day riding my bicycle on the dirt road that ran from Highway 79 beside my house to Highway 231. On this day, something Mother taught me would save my life. She taught me the rule to beware of strangers and never get in a car with anyone. I had just stopped where the dirt road intersected with Highway 79 when I saw a big blue car slow down and turn off the highway onto the dirt road. The car stopped, and I saw the man had his window down. He said, "Come and get in my car." I did not move, but I was getting scared, and my response was going to be quick. I did not say anything to the man. Then the man put a long-barrel gun out the window and said, "Get in this car, or I will shoot you." I did not have to wait until I heard him finish the sentence because as soon as I saw the gun come out of the window, I took off. My feet started turning the pedals on that bicycle as fast as they could go. In a short distance, I was at top speed. I knew by the time I got to my yard I had broken the record speed on that bicycle. I pedaled that bicycle as fast as my feet could move and then some. The man did not shoot, but he followed me out the road behind me. When I got to the back door of my house, I jumped off the bicycle, running and actually jumping through a hole at the bottom of the screen door. I was scared, and my adrenalin was pumping. Mother was in the kitchen and said, "What's wrong?" I said, "A man is trying to shoot me!" Mother looked out the door to see the car, a long blue Cadillac, driving by the house. A short time afterward, a boy was kidnapped in a nearby town and was killed. The man was caught and went to jail. I was glad mother taught me to be afraid of strangers, and I was also glad I could escape on that fast bicycle. I found out from that day that playing in the woods and on the rivers was a lot safer than being on a road. That really taught me the rule to beware of strangers.

Squirrel Dumplings and Scrambled Eggs with What?

As far back as I can remember from my childhood days, I remember Granny Woodard cooking big pans full of squirrel dumplings along with a unique side dish for anyone who wanted to try it. I would go hunting with Papa Woodard and Dad to get the squirrels. It would take six to eight squirrels for Granny Woodard to make enough dumplings for everyone. I had several cousins that were always coming by to eat at Granny Woodard's because she was a very good cook. She always had plenty of food on the table for everyone. The dinner table was at least twelve feet long, with chairs all around the table except along one wall. A long bench the length of the table was up against that wall. This bench was the place where the grandchildren would sit during meals. I remember at least ten to fifteen people eating around this table on some days. It took a lot of food to feed all these people, especially Papa Woodard. Granny Woodard had to cook in large quantities to feed the family. There were nine children in the family, and I don't know how many grandchildren. I remember when she cooked sweet potato pie, she would cook seven at a time. The story goes that one day, she cooked seven sweet potato pies and had them ready for supper. The pies did not last long because when Papa Woodard came in from the field, he ate all seven pies before he had supper.

Granny Woodard cooked all this food on a woodstove. It was the job of the grandchildren to cut the wood, split the wood into small pieces, and put it into stacks beside the woodstove for Granny to use when she cooked. It was also our job to gather up all the kindling consisting of rich pine knots to start the fire each day. We would take an ax and split the kindling and the stow wood and stack it by her woodstove to be used in cooking meals.

Other food that Granny cooked included eggs gathered from the chicken house, sausage, bacon and ham from the hogs we killed, and vegetables from the garden. Sometimes, if needed, she would open a jar of canned food she had canned earlier in the year.

Papa Woodard and Dad made syrup in the fall of the year. Papa would raise a sugarcane patch and make lots of syrup and sell it for fifty cents a gallon, but he would keep one hundred gallons to feed his family on for the winter. Papa also had around twenty bee hives, so we always had plenty of honey for the homemade biscuits, but as I remember it, we had honey and biscuits or syrup with every meal. Papa wanted Granny to cook biscuits three times a day. Also in the fall, we put sweet potatoes in a hill of pine straw and cornstalks and piled dirt to cover them to keep the sweet potatoes for the winter. With this system, we could have sweet potatoes year round. During the winter for dinner, she always had vegetables that she had canned during the summer. If it was summer, it was fresh from the garden. The spring menu was poke salad from the wild, and the fall was always lots of turnip greens from the fields. We would pull the turnips out of the ground for winter food. Some meals also consisted of food harvested from the wild. In the winter when all the hog meat was used up, the meat consisted of rabbit, squirrel, possum, quail, and plenty of catfish out of the river. Granny always had walnuts, hickory nuts, and pecans to put in the cakes and pies for desert that we all loved to eat. We always had plenty of cow's milk fresh from the cow. Other drinks included grape, scuppernong, blackberry, and tomato juice that Granny made and canned in jars. Granny was also very good at making all kinds of jellies, including strawberry, blackberry, and grape which were among her best. Add some pear and fig preserves, and it made for a good breakfast.

With these food sources, never did you hear about having to go to the store to get groceries. The only things that I ever remember Papa and Granny buying were flour and sugar and some spices from the rolling store. There was no store around, so a truck with supplies called a rolling store traveled throughout the communities. Papa carried corn to the mill to be ground into cornmeal. They definitely made it without a Walmart. This diet might be why they were so healthy in those days. They would eat a lot but would work it off in the fields raising crops, or in the woods cutting firewood and logs.

My dad taught me many tricks on how to hunt squirrels. You could still hunt and let the squirrels come out to you, or you could walk quietly through the woods to spot the squirrels. Once we spotted the squirrel in a tree, Dad would stand still while I walked around the tree to move the squirrel to the side, where my Dad would be waiting to harvest the squirrel.

As I got older, I started hunting squirrels with my slingshot. I practiced until I got very good with my slingshot. My parents would not let me have a gun at such a young age, so I became good at harvesting squirrels with my slingshot. I would use a trick my dad taught me whenever you had to hunt by yourself. I would go into the woods and gather up hickory nuts along the way and put them in my pockets until my pockets were full. When I spotted a squirrel going up a tree, I would sit beside that tree very still until I heard the squirrel coming back down the tree. This is where the hickory nuts came into use. If the squirrel came down on the other side of the tree, I would throw some hickory nuts on the other side to make noise. This would move the squirrel around to my side of the tree. This would give me a good and close shot of about ten or fifteen feet, and I was very good at that distance. Now, all I had to do was hit the squirrel in the head or neck. If you could do this several times, it would mean squirrel dumplings for supper, and Granny Woodard was always ready to cook them. As l got older, my parents let me have a gun to hunt with. Once I was able to hunt with a gun, I brought home more squirrels. As the result, Granny Woodard cooked lots of dumplings.

One day, I had very good luck hunting squirrels. So I carried all the squirrels to Granny Woodard. She was so proud to get them, for she loved to cook squirrel dumplings, but more than that, she loved the side dish that went with the dumplings. Granny helped me clean the squirrels. Now, to make the side dish, Granny would need all the squirrel brains. She washed them very good in water. She then said, "Go get some fresh eggs from the henhouse." Yes, she took the brains and eggs and scrambled them together to make her special dish, and she loved them. I have tasted them, but I was so young I can't say what they taste like, but I can say that I loved the dumplings. Everyone else loved Granny's cooking no matter what it was, and they would say that it was all good. This was the way they were raised in those days, not to waste anything. Even when we killed a hog, they did not waste one part of it. Yes, they kept the feet, skin, heart, liver, and brains to cook and prepare for a meal. My dad told me when times got tough and they ran out of meat, Granny would bake sweet potatoes and possum in the oven, and when you were hungry, it was good. I remember eating this type of food at Granny Woodard's house in my younger days. Granny Woodard was a very good cook. She was also very clean and particular.

All this food must have been very healthy because no one ever got sick back in those days. I think it was the raw cow's milk that gave us the immunity. My dad said his parents had it rough in those days, and they had to do whatever it took to survive. This meant not wasting a thing. I am so thankful we have better food today. Today's food may not be as healthy because of all the preservatives and the way it is prepared. But in those days, they were happy with whatever they could get. I believe if Granny Woodard were here today with all the good food that we have that she would still have her side dish of squirrel brains and scrambled eggs.

The Caves

As a young boy, the first I heard about caves was from some older boys that told me about the things that they had found in some local caves. We also saw pictures of caves in books at school. I was not old enough to go into them at that time, but my imagination was very intrigued from the stories that I heard from the older boys and people of the community. Some of the stories they told me were about seeing a saber-toothed tiger, monster snakes, and skeletons. Later on, I found out most of these tales were just to scare me and were not true. All these stories I heard made me want to go into a cave to see for myself.

A few years passed, and I begin to have the urge again to go into a cave. The day came when I got my first chance to go. Some neighbor boys had been in the cave that I had been hearing about for years. They invited me to go back with them, and that was all it took. I gathered up all the lights I could find, including my old, reliable carbide light. This carbide light makes a light by a flame of fire burning out of the center of a big and round reflector. The fire is fueled by carbide and water. I made sure I carried the biggest knife I owned along with a big stick. I was excited about my first chance of going into a cave, but as I was walking to the cave, I could not help thinking of the stories the older boys had told me. We even talked about the scary stories along the way. By the time we got to the cave, our imaginations were running away—thinking of what all we might find. We were sure we would find something big that we had never seen before. The stories about Native American skeletons being found in some of the caves had been talked about in the community for years. Also, we heard stories from neighbors of some very large bones being discovered there. Our state of mind was that we were going to find something too.

We were now in site of the big opening that is the entrance to the cave. Wow, the excitement and our imaginations were running wild. This would be our first cave adventure. We struck the match to light up the carbide lights to enter the cave. Not far in, I immediately saw rocks with fossils imprinted on them. Since I loved all types of rocks, I would not move from the new find for a while. Eventually, I moved on and for the first time, saw things that we had read about at school. We saw stalactites hanging from the top of the cave that had some very unusual colors. We also saw the stalagmites coming up from the floor of the cave. All of this was so new and beautiful to me. As we went farther back into the cave, we saw some rock formations created by the dripping water, connecting and making a solid rock formation. Our first cave adventure was exciting—but no saber-toothed tigers, snakes, or skeletons. Instead, we found only a few fossils and a piece of rock from the cave.

Later, we found the entrance to the cave on the other side of the mountain. Very few people knew about this entrance. The only way in was through a hole about the size of a number three wash tub. My friend and I felt we were the first to discover this side of the cave, but later we found out we may not have been the first. This cave on the other side of the mountain had small tunnels with big rocks. Some of the big rocks that were in the cave had fallen in from the ceiling. We found out from talking with older people that before they built the road, people could go in the cave on one side of the mountain and come out on the other side. Unfortunately, when they built a road over the top of the cave, the blasting caused some of the big rocks to fall in, which resulted in rocks stopping up the passageway that prevented people from going all the way through the cave.

In this "secret" part of the cave, we found our first real danger. After entering, we walked along a ledge above a very deep hole to get to the back of a room inside the cave. We shined our lights from the ledge to see if we could see the bottom of the hole, but we could not. The light could not shine to the bottom, so we decided to throw rocks off the ledge to see how deep it was. Unbelievably, we counted to four or five before the rocks hit the bottom of the hole.

At the bottom of the hole was a pool of water. We had fun throwing rocks off into that deep hole and listening to the rocks hit the water way down deep. We never thought about it at the time, but if we would have fallen in, we would have been gone. Thankfully, we were kept safe. We went into these caves several times looking for whatever we could find, which resulted in nothing but a few memories and some fossils.

We continued looking for new caves. We knew of another cave about five miles from my house that people told us about. Several people told us of going through the cave and coming out on the other side in the top of the mountain. Once we heard of this, we had to do it. Several of us decided one day that we would go into this cave, which had several passageways where you could easily get lost. We were able to reach our goal of going all the way through and coming out at the top of the mountain on several occasions. This was a very fun cave to explore. It was especially fun when a large group went and we divided up to explore new passageways or play hide and seek. Because someone would always get lost, we would yell to find one another until everybody was found before we left the cave. What luck we had that everyone was always found and kept safe.

Now, the last cave I explored was the biggest, the scarcest, and the most dangerous. In the other caves, you may go in under the mountain a half mile, or no more than three quarters of a mile underground. This last cave was much longer. If you went in at one o'clock in the afternoon, you would not get out till dark. It would take you three hours to get to the back of the cave. You had to be able to climb a rope up and down because this was the only way to enter the cave. At the entrance, you had to climb down about twenty-five feet of rope into a big room. We tied the rope to a tree and threw it in and climbed down. Once in, it was a long journey walking and climbing over rocks and water to get to the back of the cave. We traveled a long way back in under the mountain, maybe over a mile. This cave did not come out on the other side of the mountain; it only went down deep in the ground. As we traveled through with about two hours of walking and climbing over rocks and water in the cave the ceiling started to get lower toward the floor. One thing that I saw in the cave that I had never seen before was the fish and crayfish did not have any eyes. This cave was full of massive stalactites and stalagmites with unbelievable colors. We also found lots of fossils. As the ceiling got closer to the floor, it got to the point that you had to crawl. We crawled at least two or three hundred yards through an opening about two feet tall and twenty feet wide on our stomachs. The ceiling was right against my back as I crawled. Finally, we reached a big room the size of a football field with a high ceiling of maybe, a hundred feet. This was a massive room for a cave, the biggest one I had ever been in until later in my adult years when I visited some nationally known caves with tour guides. The long crawl was worth it; we now had been to a place very few people had ever been. I returned a couple of times to the cave to explore new passageways, but I finally had enough.

The four caves that I explored as a youth were all different. Some of these trips were for adventure, some for challenges, and some were just very dangerous. We never found any saber tooth tigers, monster snakes, or skeletons. I think back to the dangers that we were exposed to and know we all had to be lucky that we did not get hurt or lost in one of these caves. The biggest danger was the bats in the caves. The things that scare me the most today is how deep that hole was; the other is the tight space we were in during the time we crawled to the big room. The last danger was being under a mountain more than a mile down without anyone knowing our location. These are things you do when you are young, and you do them without thinking.

We never found anything of value in any of these caves. All we got for all the adventures were memories and the thought that we had been where very few people dared to go. I am glad to have these memories from my younger days in life—and thank God for watching over us during these adventures and keeping us all safe.

The Wind Saved My Life

It was July, and my uncle was getting two weeks of vacation. He wanted me to help run trotlines on the Warrior River to try our luck at catching big catfish. All the crops were laid by, it was raining every day, and all the work had been done, so my dad said it would be okay for me to go with him. My dad also decided he could build us a boat out of some old poplar lumber that he had sawed and stored down in the barn. My dad made this boat so we could fish and run trotlines. I remember all the nails going into the boat. I remember the black tar they used to seal up the cracks where the boards fit together. They also rubbed the boat down with bees wax so it would repel water. We were so proud we had a boat because most of the time, we would wade the river or ride on an inner tube in a sitting position to run the lines in deep water. This was a great little boat. When we first put the boat in the river, it didn't even leak, although that would not be the case in later years.

We had good luck fishing for the first few days. We caught some big catfish and some giant gar. Some of the gar was as long as I was tall. We were having the time of our lives. My little cousin was only about six years old, but he went along on every fishing trip with us. I was a very good swimmer, and I thought that if the boat went down, I could save him. I am also sure his daddy thought the same.

The little boat was working to perfection for a homemade boat. My uncle had a little 5-hp Johnson motor that he put on the back of the boat. This motor would push the boat six or seven miles per hour up and down the river. Boy, were we having fun fishing and riding in this little homemade boat.

One afternoon, we gathered our bait and headed for the river, the same as we had done for several days in a row. This day would be different. We parked our truck under a big oak tree in a big flat spot on the bank of the river. We put the boat into the water and traveled to where we wanted to put our lines out. We began to put the trotlines across the river. After the second line was finished, we headed up the river about a mile to put another line across the river. We heard a thunder in the north, and a cloud was coming up, but we were not afraid of clouds that much. We thought the cloud might go around us, so we continued on with baiting the lines until the last hook was baited. We were about a mile up the river from the truck. The big trees were tall and leaning out over the river, so our vision of the cloud was blocked. We could see that it was getting very dark, and the thunder and lightning were getting very close. So we headed for the truck at the fastest speed the little Johnson motor would push us. We were out in the middle of the river when the cloud hit us. My little cousin was so small

I thought the wind was going to blow him out of the boat. So I put him in front of me and wrapped him up in an old poncho we had in the boat and held him down. It was raining so hard that it was filling up the boat. The wind was blowing the rain sideways and hitting us with its great force. The thunder and lightning were over our heads. The storm was on top of us.

Then, a lightning bolt hit a tree. *Kaboom.* We could see the truck three hundred yards away, but suddenly, the wind changed directions. Now, it was blowing against us, right in our face. The water was white-capping. The little Johnson motor was wide-open and was doing all it could do to push the boat, but the wind was very strong and rough. We almost came to a standstill because the wind was blowing so hard toward us, but we were getting closer to the truck. With the wind and rain blowing in our face and the boat filling with water from the downpour of rain, we were now moving very slowly. It was dark, and we could barely see ahead of us. We were now within yards of the truck, thinking safety was near, when a big lightning bolt hit the oak tree that the truck was parked under. The ball of fire ran the big oak tree and then arced over the river into the sky. It appeared the sky was on fire for a second, and I will never forget that sight.

Now we were scared! We didn't know what we were going to do. It was raining so hard the boat was filling with water, and we were wet to the bone. However, there was nothing else to do but try to get to the truck and go home. Finally, we made it to the truck. Thankfully, neither the tree nor its falling limbs hit the truck. We pulled the boat up onto the bank. I helped my little cousin out of the boat and put him into the truck. My uncle got the motor off the boat, and I tied the boat to a tree so we would have the boat there the next morning to check our lines. So we went home to put on dry clothes and eat some good food. We told everyone how fortunate we were to get out of that storm alive.

The next morning, we went back to check our lines, but not before getting a little lecture from my mother about the weather. The river was high, and the water was up to the tree where I had tied the boat the day before. That made it very dangerous to be in the little boat with the rapidly moving muddy water. However, we were determined to check our lines for catfish. The first line was completely washed away by the rapid water and floating logs going down the river. The second line had some big catfish on it, so we began to gather them into the boat because that is what fishing was all about.

We headed up the river to check the last trotline. This trotline was stretched all the way across the river. The first side of the river that we went to, we checked the line, and it had broken away from the limb. So we crossed the river to the other side. Good, the line was still there. We took a few fish off the line, and then I felt something that felt like a big log hung on the line. The line was going back and forth in the swift, muddy water, but I couldn't see what it was. I thought that it must have been a log because a fish couldn't have been that big. We pulled the weighted line closer to the boat. A few feet from the boat, I told my uncle, "I think this just might be a fish."

About that time, a big five-foot-long yellow catfish rolled to the surface. Wow, that was a giant of a fish! The fish rolled and then dove down deep in the water. I pulled on the fish but could not move him. Suddenly, he pulled the line right out of my hands. My uncle also had the line in his hand, so he tried to get the big fish up. The fish rolled on the surface, twisting and turning. My uncle tried to pull the fish into the boat, but the fish was half the length of our little homemade boat. We had a dip net, but the fish would not fit in it. The fish made another deep dive, pulling the line out of my uncle's hand. He said, "If I had not let go of the line, the fish would have turned the boat over." We could not get the fish in the boat, so we went back to the bank where the line was tied, and now, we would try to pull the fish toward the bank so we could get this monster yellow cat on the riverbank. As we were pulling the fish in, his fight was very strong. As he got closer to the bank, he made another big run, straightened the hook, and escaped to freedom. That was the biggest fish we ever hung in all of our years of fishing on the river.

It was a great two weeks of fishing and adventure on the river. I stayed wet the whole time, got very little sleep, and my hands were sore from baiting hooks and taking fish off the trotlines. We cleaned all the fish, kept some for ourselves, and gave some to our neighbors. We had a great time, and now, we have good memories from the adventures. Mother reminds us of how God took care of us on that day and many others. We used the boat for many years on the river. That little boat Dad made for us and the fun we had with it created some of my best memories as a boy.

I think back to the storm, and remember how the wind changing direction and blowing in our face against our little homemade boat, which slowed the boat to an almost standstill, saved our lives. If we had maintained our same speed all the way to the truck, we would have made it to the truck about the same time the lightning bolt hit the tree. We probably would have all been killed. I believe to this day that the wind changing direction saved our lives. What ever happened on that day was meant to be, and I am thankful that fate worked out to give us another day on this earth. Thank God for watching over us.

The Day I Ran Faster than Ever

I had won the junior high county track meet for the one-hundred yard dash, but on the day I broke my own record, no one was around to time me. It was a rainy day, and as usual, my thoughts turned to looking for arrowheads after school. A friend, who was also a fast runner, was looking in this field for arrowheads and had told me about being chased out of the field by a man. After school, we were both looking for arrowheads and saw the man coming into the field, so we took off running, and he did not catch us. I don't think he owned the land, he just farmed it. At one time, I was given permission to hunt the land by a family member, so I thought it was okay for me to be in that field.

On another afternoon after getting home from school, I made my way to a place that I thought I might find some arrowhead points. It was the field adjacent to where we had been chased out by the farmer. I was very alert while looking for points. I kept one eye on the ground looking for points and the other eye looking for the man that might be trying to catch us.

For some reason, I didn't invite my friend to go hunting with me that day, so I was by myself. I felt that if I saw the man, I could just outrun him. I had hunted for a short while and was finding some points when I let my guard down. I walked down the corn row to the end of the row next to the woods, and I turned around and started back on the next row when I felt something behind me. I looked around, and the man was right behind me, about two feet—with his pistol pointed in my back. Wow, I had never been in this position before! He had been hiding in the bushes, and when I turned around to walk the next row of corn, he then snuck up right behind me. He said, "Stop, I don't want you in this field. I want you to walk to the edge of the field and leave."

I followed his instructions. I can't remember exactly what I said, but I think I said, "I thought I had permission from your wife." He walked behind me with the pistol in my back. He said, "If I catch you in this field again, I will shoot you." I was really scared. After getting to the edge of the field, he told me, "You better get out of here before I shoot you." And I think he said, "I am counting to ten, and then I am going to start shooting." Anyway, when he let me go, I broke my record in the one-hundred yard dash, two-hundred yard dash, four-hundred yard dash, and any other distance you'd care to measure. I did not stop running till I got home, which was a little over a mile.

I told Mother what happened, and she was very upset. When my dad got home from work, I told him what happened, and he was not happy. He put me in the truck and carried me to the man's house. He told the

man, "That was no way to do to scare a boy like that!"
Dad told him he had better not ever do that again. He
was very upset with the man and told him a few more
things that he was not happy with, especially his actions
against me. He told him he better apologize to me, and
the man did tell me he was sorry. Then Dad said to me,
"You don't need to be back over in that field ever again!" I
never did hunt arrowheads in that field again.

Chains and Billy Sticks

On one Saturday night when I was thirteen, I went into town with my eighteen-year-old brother, who was home, on leave. He had joined the U. S. Marines and had been in training for sixteen weeks. He went through eight weeks of basic training and eight more weeks of special hand-to-hand combat training. They were preparing him to be able to fight in any situation. He was home for a few days before he had to be shipped out to Vietnam. We were glad to have him home. So that Saturday evening, he asked if I wanted to go to town with him. I was young and proud to be riding around with a U. S. Marine, and I wanted to spend all the time I could with my brother before he left. I had not been on many trips to town with my brother because I was young, and he had been known to get into a few scrapes in the past.

On this night, I did not have a clue that there would be a fight. We had just planned to ride around and see some of his friends and then go home before he had to leave for the Vietnam War. We had only been in town for a short time when we pulled into a parking space down the street from the movie theater. We got out and started walking toward the theater. I don't know why, but I think he must have seen some girls that he wanted to talk to. I was just following along behind him, happy to have the chance to tag along.

We only walked a few feet when he turned to me and told me to get back in the truck and lock the door! Instantly, I saw five guys running down the street toward us. Following his instructions, I ran quickly and got in the truck and locked the door. That was the best move I ever made. My brother ran in front of the truck with these guys chasing him. One guy came to my side and tried to open the door but could not get in. I had never been in this situation before, and I didn't know how I had gotten in this one. These five guys had billy sticks and two-foot-long chains. I figured we were doomed.

When my brother got to his truck door, he turned to fight. I saw him hit those guys and knock them to the pavement. The guy on my side goes in front of the truck to join the fight, and within seconds, my brother knocked him flat on his back. Within minutes, my brother had whipped all five guys and was now getting in the truck when one guy came for my brother's truck door handle. The boy was met with a truck door to his head and appeared to be knocked out. My brother started the truck, and we took off. I looked back to see some guys lying in the street with a couple of the boys standing over the others checking their injuries. The truck was now moving at a high speed, and when we hit the long stretch of the road, we reached the speed of ninety miles per hour. I don't think my Dad's 1955 Ford pickup truck had ever been driven that fast, and I certainly had never been in a vehicle going anywhere near that fast.

I had never been in this situation before, and I was a little scared. My brother traveled out of town until he hit the back roads, going through Swan Bridge and across McCoy Mountain and then off the roads to a big field where we waited for hours. He thought someone might have tried to follow him. After we figured it was safe and no one was looking for us anymore, he drove home.

The next morning, we had the county deputy in our front yard because someone in town had identified him and given his name to the deputy. The deputy told us some of the boys had to go to the hospital. They questioned my brother, and he told them what happened. He explained that he was attacked by chains and clubs and it was self defense. He told the deputy he only had what the marines had taught him. He said that he was the property of the U. S. Marines and he was going to Vietnam the next week. They did not arrest him and agreed that it was self-defense. Not only did he survive two tours in Vietnam, but on that Saturday night, he whipped all five guys and got in the truck and drove off and not one guy ever hit him. I was really young, but I knew one thing for sure: I did not want to ever get in that situation again.

Addendum

I did want to recognize my brother and his service to our country in the U. S. Marines. Below is one of his stories from Vietnam. Please be advised that the following deals with a much more serious and harsh subject matter than the rest of the book.

My brother went on to Vietnam and served two tours and engaged in many fights that made our Saturday night brawl seem like a cakewalk. My brother had many narrow escapes in Vietnam and was wounded. He served on fifty-seven rescue missions. On one of these missions, fifteen men from his unit were sent into Cambodia to rescue two pilots that were shot down. Only five men and the two pilots returned alive. While on this rescue mission, he had many occasions that were close calls. Some of the men were killed before they reached the pilot. One of my brother's friends took a .50 caliber machine gun with a 1000-round clip and charged the enemy, killing many of them to try to save the unit because he could not take it anymore. He went down after taking nine bullets.

After they reached the pilots, they came under heavy fire, and they used all the ammunition they had. He was down to his last strap when they dug a hole and buried themselves alive. They used bamboo sticking up out of the ground to breathe from. He said he always kept a bamboo stick in his backpack because it had saved his life many times. After they buried themselves underground, they called the planes to drop napalm on top of them, which is fire that wipes out everything above ground. Under fire and outnumbered by the enemy, this was the only way out. The planes wiped the enemy out with gunfire and napalm. After the fire was clear, they dug out and proceeded to walk three miles by night to make it inside the pickup zone. The entire mission was travel by night and bury in the ground, or hiding under water breathing through a bamboo stick during daylight hours. Five of the men took turns carrying on their backs the two wounded pilots a distance of about three miles to the Vietnamese border where they were supposed to be picked up by helicopters. Before they were rescued by the helicopters, they came under fire again, and they played dead in a rice field that was full of water and, again, breathed through a bamboo stick for hours before the helicopters came to pick them up.

They did get the pilots out alive but lost ten of the fifteen men doing it. We were proud he made it back alive, and we thanked him for his service. Many of his friends and our cousin did not make it back alive. In my cousin's unit of 180 men, all were killed except fifteen men who were wounded. My brother's convoy of fourteen trucks, two jeeps, and one hundred men were trying to get to them with food, supplies, and rescue, but they were under enemy fire also. They were trying to get to them, and they were within three miles from the rescue when my cousin's unit was wiped out.

The U.S. Marines had really trained my brother to fight well, survive extreme conditions, and perform like a U. S. Marine. With God watching over him, he made it back alive. Like my brother said, "A bullet just didn't have his name on it."

Bright Lights, Bullets, and the High-Speed Chase

I was a senior in high school, and we didn't have much to do on Saturday nights except to ride around on back roads and look for deer. We did not have a gun or have any intention of killing one. We were just riding around to see if we could see one. Deer had just been stocked in the county two years earlier, and it was rare to see one. Although I had seen three deer cross our field a year earlier, which was the first time I had ever seen a deer, they were still a very rare sight. Prior to deer being stocked in our area in the late '60s, there had been no deer for many years. They had been wiped out by disease several decades earlier.

The deer season in our area had not yet been opened for hunting; it was still a year away. As a matter of fact, the only deer hunt I had ever been on at this time was when the booster club paid the way for the football team to go hunting in south Alabama for a three-day hunt. This was a reward to our team for having such a great year. There I saw my first deer in the woods while hunting. It was a beautiful doe, and I enjoyed seeing her in the wild, but on this hunt, only bucks were allowed to be shot. I did not kill or see any bucks on this hunt.

Only a few people would ride the roads to kill a deer. Most people just wanted to see one because it was something rare that we never had before in our county. But when someone did kill a deer at night from the road, it made the landowners very mad. One night, someone killed my girlfriend's father's prize bull. Now, that made him very upset at spotlighters. (People that killed deer from the road were called spotlighters.) The next time he saw a car come down the road spotlighting, he jumped in his truck and chased the boys down and made them hand over the spotlight to him. He told them never to spotlight his land again, or he would have them arrested. He kept the spotlight and used it on the farm for years. He protected the deer because the first deer to be stocked in the county, four does and two bucks, were released on his farm, and he and his family enjoyed watching them run and play. Most people and the landowners wanted to protect the deer.

One night, we were riding around looking for deer. We did not have a spotlight or gun because it was against the law, and we were not planning on killing one. We were just riding around using our headlights from our truck, hoping we would see a deer on the side of the road, or see one as it crossed the road. We did not want to harm a deer. My best friend and my cousin were riding with me on this night. I turned down this back road which was a narrow, dirt road, and all of a sudden, bright lights were turned on us. I began to back out to the main road as fast as I could. We had our windows rolled down in the truck because it was a warm fall night. About the time we got backed up onto the main road, we heard gun fire. The truck with the bright lights was shooting at us! I put the pedal to the metal and spun out as fast as I could go.

My cousin said, "I just heard a bullet go by my ear!" I did hear the bullets going over the top of the truck. I was flying on that dirt road. I am sure we broke record speed on that road because I had the gas pedal to the floor. The truck chased us for a short distance, but we were able to outrun him and lose him on some back roads. We had escaped to safety, and we were all breathing a little easier. I was afraid the truck might have a bullet hole in the side, so we stopped at a safe location after we were sure we were no longer being followed to check the truck out. Thank goodness, no bullet holes in the truck. I am also glad we didn't have any in us! The man was shooting over our truck to scare us, and he did. If the man wanted to hit us or our truck, he could have. I am so glad he decided to shoot over our truck instead of shooting into our truck.

I found out later that someone had killed a deer on this man's property at night, and he was very mad about it. He also did not want anyone shooting toward his cattle. If I had known that, I would not have been riding around on that road. As a landowner, we have had people to kill deer off our property in daytime and at night, without permission to hunt. I now know, as I am much older, and understand the feeling that man had on that night. He was only trying to protect the deer as I do today. But we got the scare of our life, and we did not turn down that road ever again.

The Big Catch at Scirum Bluff

It was dark nights in July, and this was one of the best times to catch a big catfish. I was about sixteen years old and had already had some exciting fishing adventures on the Locust Fork of the Warrior River. But as far as this trip went, it was one time we set a record catching several big catfish. We had caught some good bait the few days before this fishing trip. We had a basket full of crawfish and some giant creek minnows along with a bag of chicken livers and fiddle worms. The river was low and clear, but what we had going for us was that we had some good bait, and it was the dark nights in July. We decided to head for Scirum Bluff, a place where we had always caught lots of fish.

We had been there many times before. Scirum Bluff was on the Locust Fork of the Warrior River and provided some great fishing for us during our young life. It had a big deep hole of water with a long high bluff. The water would go way back up under the bluff's overhang. Some skin divers that had been in it underwater said it was like a big cave opening that went deep back under the bluff. They also had spotted some big catfish under the bluff.

We planned to use inner tubes to ride on in a sitting position to put the trotlines running right up under the bluff in the deep water. The trotlines would run along under the bluff a distance of about two hundred yards.

Putting the trotlines in, we saw plenty of snakes. Some of the rock ledges were full of snakes, and there were several on limbs hanging out over the water. Some snakes were as big as my arm. My uncle told me if you shake the limb and make the snake fall in the water, it could not bite you underwater. I must have believed him because there were snakes everywhere, but I was not scared of them after he told me that. I figured that if they were up on a limb or rock, they would not hurt me and if they were underwater, they couldn't bite me, and I was good with that. Later on as an adult, I knew better. He was just trying to get me to not be afraid. I later heard of a person who was bitten underwater and died. Then, I began to think a little differently.

On the trotline, we had short lines about a foot long, which hung down from the main line with a hook on them. These short lines were put about every three or four feet, with bait on the hooks. We would alternate baiting the trotlines using minnows, worms, crawfish, and chicken livers, until we ran out of bait. We baited up the trotlines right before dark, with plans to come back and run our lines at twelve o'clock that night. We went to the house to get something to eat, with plans to head back to the river and be there by ten. We fished with our rods and reels from the sandy side of Scirum, and caught several four and five-pounders using fiddle worms for bait.

Soon, it was twelve o'clock, and it was time to check the trotlines. I could not see my hand in front of my face without a light because it was so dark. It would be especially dark up under the bluff. Our main source of light was carbide lights. We got into our inner tubes, and started paddling with our hands across the 150-yard wide deep hole of water. With me were my uncle, and, of course, my little cousin that was only about seven years old. We paddled toward our trotlines over and under the bluff with great anticipation of having some big fish on our lines. We were not worried about snakes now because we couldn't even see them.

When my uncle got to the place where we tied the trotline to a limb which hung out over the water, we could see the limb going up and down. We had a big fish on the first hook. My uncle reached down, got the first monster yellow catfish in the mouth, and I put him on the stringer. The catfish weighed over fifteen pounds. Wow, this one fish was bouncing my inner tube up and down in the water and pulling me all around! That was just the beginning; the next three or four fish we took off the line were seven and eight pound blue catfish. Out in the middle on the trotline was the biggest yellow catfish! It was a real task to get this twenty-pound yellow catfish under control and on the stringer, but we did.

By then, I had so much weight hanging on my inner tube that it was mostly underwater. I wasn't sure I could get all of the fish to the bank. We took some more four and five-pounders off the trotline and added them to the stringer. We only carried one stringer to put the fish on, and it was almost full. I started paddling across the

Scirum hole of the water, and because of the weight from the fish, I was barely moving. Occasionally, I could feel a powerful pull from one of the big fish on the string. As I was paddling across the Scirum hole of water, I was sometimes bobbing up and down from the forceful pulls of the fish trying to escape to deep water. After paddling for a long time trying to pull the heavy string of fish, I was successful in reaching the sandy white banks where the truck was parked. The fish we caught on the rods and reels plus the ones taken off the trotlines were a record catch. It was a massive stringer of yellow and blue catfish that I will always remember.

Our cotton scales only went to one hundred pounds. When we got home to weigh the fish on the cotton scales, it maxed out at one hundred pounds, and all the weight of the large stringer of fish pulled the needle all the way to the bottom. So we never knew how much all the fish actually weighed. We just knew we had lots of fun, and now, we have the memories of that exciting fishing adventure on that dark July night on the Warrior River at Scirum Bluff.

Pea Patch Advice

There was a very fine lady that worked on our farm for several years. She had it hard, the same as a lot of people back in my childhood days. She would help us plant, hoe, and gather all the crops. She would wash all the vegetables, put them in baskets or sacks, and load the truck for the farmers' market. She was a very hard worker. She would go to work in a field all day by herself, and you never had to worry about if she would get the job done. She was a lady that worked for us, but was always telling me what I needed to do. For example, she would say, "You better plow your tomatoes" or "You better spray your peas, or they're going to be wormy."

In other words, she was on top of our farming operation, plus she liked giving me advice. On the other hand, after working in the field all day long, if she saw my mother hanging clothes out on the line, she would be right over there helping. She was one of the best neighbors you could ever have: honest as the day was long and always willing to help others. Over the years, she became more than a neighbor. She became more like family. Mother would always say, "Wouldn't it be nice if everyone in the world was like her?"

Her husband was also self-employed. He was a professional with a slingshot. He made and sold slingshots for a living. In those days, slingshots were in high demand, and everyone had or wanted a slingshot made by "Slingshot Shorty," as he was called. If you made your own slingshot, you had to buy the rubber bands from him because he had the super strong ones, and you could not get them anywhere else. He would also teach people how to shoot their slingshot, and he taught me a great deal. He was very good, and no one could beat him at shooting. He could shoot a steel ball down the neck of a Coke bottle and knock the bottom out, and he could shoot a sewing thread in two pieces from ten yards away. He would go on shooting exhibitions, and he amazed everyone with his shooting skills.

I had been dating a girl for a while, and we had decided we would get married. So one day, I was working in the pea patch alongside my neighbor, and I told her that I was going to get married. She told me, "I am only going to give you one bit of advice about that, you can take it or leave it. I married Shorty and thought we would live on love. After seven days, we were about to starve to death, and we had to go to work. We have been working ever since, and you better get ready to do the same! You better enjoy your youth while you can." I have thought about that statement over the years and understand how true that statement is. Her statement is so true for every young couple that plans on getting married, and it contains much wisdom. You have to work on every aspect of marriage, from raising children to making enough money to make it work and provide for the family. She was so right! The pea patch advice was words of wisdom that are so true.

Wagon on the Barn Roof

A man in the community woke up one morning, looked off his porch towards his barn, and to his amazement, his wagon was sitting on top of his barn. He panicked because this was his only means of transportation. In those days, everyone traveled in a wagon. He believed some force of nature put his wagon up on the barn for a reason. He thought it could be a sign from a higher power. He walked to get some of his neighbors to come witness the wagon on top of the barn. He proceeded to tell them that this was some kind of sign. This man was one who believed the earth was flat and the stars in the sky were eyes watching down on us, among many other strange beliefs. He told the neighbors the wagon weighed over five hundred pounds, and it was not humanly possible for any one person to put that wagon on top of the barn.

Sitting on top of the barn, the wagon straddled the barn's ridge, with wheels on each side. The wagon was completely intact, and was positioned right in the center of the top of the barn. The neighbors told him someone had to put the wagon up there, which made him very angry. He wanted to know who put it up there and how in the world would anyone be able to get a wagon up there.

He never found out who put the wagon on top of the barn. But the neighbors being good neighbors, as they were back in those days, did pitch in to help him take the wagon apart and lower the pieces down one at a time with a rope. The neighbors put his wagon back together again on the ground, and then they all had a good laugh about the prank, wondering how in the world someone could come up with that idea. Once the man had seen the wagon taken apart and reassembled on the ground, he understood how it was able to be put on his barn roof. The man was very appreciative of his neighbors for helping to get the wagon down and restore it back together on the ground.

Boys in the community with nothing to do one moonlit night came up with the idea to take this man's wagon apart and put it back together again on top of his barn. They were able to do it without being caught or waking him up. It took the boys all night to pull off this wagon prank. Other pranks the boys would pull in the older days were setting up a dumbbar at people's houses at night. A dumbbar was made out of a long beeswax string, which was tied to a big bucket or barrel. As you rubbed your hand or a corncob across this string, it would make a very loud noise that sounded very weird and scary. It would usually wake the people up wondering what in the world could make such a scary noise. Sometimes, the people would come out of the house with a shotgun and start shooting, and all the boys would run. All of these boys grew up and served our country in World War II and returned to our county as heroes, good citizens, and leaders in our community. One of those boys was my dad. These pranks were not intended to hurt anyone, but it did give the young boys things to do for entertainment back in those days.

The Unexplained Force

As far back as I can remember in my childhood, I had a dream of hunting in the woods like the Native Americans. As a child, I loved going to the woods for adventures and imagining that I was a Native American. I remember pretending that I had an imaginary friend, who was Native American, with me during these adventures. I would run through the woods by myself playing, running from tree to tree, and at times, I would imagine that I would see a tribe of Native Americans. This just seemed like childhood play and the imagination we have as children growing up. We did not have a television to learn these things. We would learn about the Native Americans at school, or hear these stories from parents and family. I was always fascinated with stories and information about Native Americans. It seemed there was always a force driving me to want to learn more.

At a very young age, I learned how to make a bow and arrow. My dad helped me make the bow from a small hickory tree. I spent many hours carving on the hickory stick to make it into a bow. Remember, we did not have a television or video games, so we had plenty of time to make the things we wanted and needed because we did not have the money to buy them. I found a long, strong string and rubbed it with beeswax to make it smooth for my bowstring. I made my arrows from any type of straight stick I could find, although that was a challenge sometimes. We had chickens and turkeys, so finding the feathers for the arrows was not a problem. I shot my bow and arrow all the time, and I learned that if I heated the points of the arrows, which was the end of the stick sharpened with a knife, it would make them harder. I shot the arrows into boxes and other targets, but occasionally, I would lose one.

On one occasion, I found one of these arrows unexpectedly while running through the yard barefooted. The arrow was under the grass, but the sun had caused it to curl up, just enough for the point to be sticking up. As I was running through the yard playing, my foot hit the arrow—causing it to stick through my foot. The arrow stuck all the way through my foot, leaving four to six inches sticking out of the top of my foot. I yelled for Mother! My mother came, and she panicked. She tried to pull the arrow out, and I yelled because it hurt so much. I knew Mother was strong enough to pull it out, but for some reason, she could not. She told me to wait because Dad would be in from work in a few minutes, and he would be able to get it out.

It seemed like a long time passed. We did not have a phone, and also, there was no such thing as 911 in those days. Mother could not drive at that time. Besides, we only had one truck, and Dad was driving it coming in from work. Dad finally got home and immediately pulled the arrow out of my foot. My foot had a hole in it, so he immediately poured some coal oil on it because that was what everyone did for cuts back in those days. I remember it really did burn. He also put some Rally Salve on it.

I went to school on Monday, and the swelling got so big that my foot was too big for my shoe. That afternoon when I got home from school, I showed Mother my foot. Mother said, "When your Dad gets home from work, we are going to take you to the doctor in Oneonta." We went to the doctor that evening, and I was put in the hospital for a week because of the infection. It healed up, but I still have the scar in the top of my foot today.

I continued perfecting my skills with the bow and arrow, and I had some amazing adventures in the woods, hunting with my bow. My mother was always amazed at what I might bring home with me. For example, one day, I brought her a groundhog. I was so proud of the accomplishment, but she was not at all happy. All of the adventures that I had in the woods as a child were of imagination, fascination, and the unexplained.

Years later, sometime in my late teens, my mother told us that our Papa Jesse was half or three-quarters Cherokee. I was very intrigued with that statement. I was so proud to find out that I was really part Cherokee. By the time I started to college, I had acquired a lot of knowledge about the Native American way of life, especially the Cherokee. I also began to study about artifacts and ancient tools and learned as much as I could about the ways in which the Native American tools were used for survival by the Native American people, especially in Alabama.

It was not until I was an adult that my mother told me the full story of the heritage of our family that had been passed down through generations. She started out by saying, "This is not pretty to talk about, and this is the way it was told to me by my daddy, Aunt Ruthie, and Aunt Ida." Then she said, "My daddy's great-grandmother was a Cherokee. She became pregnant with a white man's baby. The Cherokee tribe did not believe in mixed blood, so this was not allowed in the tribe. The fate of the Cherokee girl after having the baby was unknown, but it was told that she was put to death. The baby was taken by leaders of the Cherokee tribe to a family that had the name Keener. The young boy was given the name Bud Keener by the Keener family that took him in." Mother always referred to him as Grandpa Keener. This was my mother's great-grandfather. As the story goes, he married a Cherokee girl, and they had one daughter named Liz Keener, who was Papa Jesse's mother and my mother's grandmother. Liz would marry a man by the name of Bud Johns. He was known to have some Cherokee in his ancestors. Liz would have a very rough time. They had three children: Ruth, Allie, and Jesse. Jesse was my grandfather, who we called Papa Jesse.

One day, more bad luck would hit the family. Bud left the home and did not return. Not a word was ever heard from him after that day. To this day, no one knows if he just left home or if he got killed or died from natural causes somewhere. Liz was left with three children to raise and feed by herself. There was no welfare, no government assistance, and no one to help them. It made it hard for them to survive. After almost starving to death and things looking hopeless, Liz carried the children down to the river to drown them, but Papa Jessie looked up to her with his big brown eyes, and she looked into his eyes. After that, she said her heart would not let her do it.

Not knowing what she was going to do, she started walking and caught a ride on a wagon traveling to Straight Mountain to the only family she knew: Jesse and Ruthie Phillips. It was very difficult for women to make it and provide for three children without a man to help in those days. She had no way of providing for or feeding the three children or herself. After living with Jesse and Ruthie Phillips for a short time, she eventually met and married a man we called Grandpa Green, who also had three children, and he was Ruthie's older brother. After their marriage, they tried raising the children together, but it did not work out because she said Grandpa Green was not good to her children. So she gave her first three children back to Jesse and Ruthie Phillips, who did not have any children of their own but who could care and provide for them. Later, Liz and Grandpa Green did have seven children of their own. Their names were Herman, George, Ida, Elbert, Katie, Freddie, and Martha Ann Green.

What a tough time this family had for several generations during those days. Papa Jesse grew up and was thought to be very smart. Jesse Phillips wanted him to go to school to become a doctor, but he married Mary Haynes instead. They had ten children, with the third oldest being my mother. Their names were Lilly, Vernon, Annie Mae, James, Edward, Mary Ruth, Orland, Benny, Bonnie, Donnie. Vernon was called Odie and Edward was called Deedy. After Uncle Jesse Phillips passed away, Aunt Ruthie came and lived with Jesse and Mary Johns, who were my grandparents. My mother said she told them many stories of her family and the history of the family. She helped raise my mother and her brothers and sisters, and my mother said, "Everyone loved her dearly." She was loved and respected by the family and the community and was dearly missed when she passed.

Papa Jesse was always considered to be like a doctor in ways because he would always doctor the children with natural homemade remedies. He used some Native American medicine along with other natural medicine to doctor his children. He used blackberries and boiled blackberry roots to treat the sick, mainly for the stomachache and diarrhea. He believed in using yellow root for sore throats and bad colds; and sassafras tea was a cure for all. If that didn't work, a little castor oil to work you out would take care of the rest. At last for cuts, aches and pain, or sore muscles, a little Rally Salve would be the treatment. For him, a little homemade wine and home brew was the treatment. His family knew that he went several times a year to visit Native American tribes and people that were probably related to him. He learned some of the medicinal remedies from his visits with the Native American people. He told his children and grandchildren to be proud of their Indian heritage because he was very proud of his Native American blood.

This story may have the answer to the unexplained: of why the force pulled me to the rivers, creeks, caves, and woods during my life. I have always loved nature and the beauty it reveals. I still, to this day, love to learn about Native Americans and their way of life and survival. I really love being close to nature and enjoying the beauty of each season. Did the adventures and imagination as a child have some connection with the past, or was it just a child growing up on a farm with no television or video games but with a big imagination? No one knows for sure. The woods, creeks, rivers, caves, and our imagination provided us entertainment and adventures in those days as a young boy. I look back now to the memories with some questions to why all this happened. There is no explanation for some of it, except it was just meant to be the path we all had to take to reach our destination in life.

The Coon That Thought My Cousin Was a Tree

When I was a young man, I loved to coon hunt. I liked the adventures, the excitement, and the unexpected. I loved to train the dogs and listen to a good black and tan hound run a coon over the hills, hollows, creeks, and rivers of this county. My cousins had some blue tick hounds, but the black and tan was my favorite. The best dog I owned was a black and tan hound named Old Blue. He had a great voice that you could hear him from a long way off. His howl was long like *bahooooooooo* until he treed a coon. Then he would let you know that the coon was treed with a short voice like *yok yok yok*. We had many adventures like the time on Austin Creek when he treed a coon in a hole after a long race under a bluff.

My cousin had the ability to call a coon out of a hole, or sometimes, even call them down a tree. He would do this by using a coon squall. On this occasion, he got down on his hands and knees with his nose about two feet from the hole. He began squalling like a coon. After about two minutes, the coon came right out of the hole, and for the challenge, my cousin was face to face with this big old coon. The coon won the battle very quickly. My cousin jumped up, and the coon ran right between his legs, which was really a funny sight to see. My cousin has not moved that fast since then.

We had some young dogs at the time, so I turned them loose first and held Old Blue back. The coon won the battle quickly with those young dogs. Then I turned Old Blue loose, and the fight was over. After many coon hunting trips and many exciting adventures, Blue got old. I traded him to my cousin for an old-timer pocket knife. I knew he would take care of him. Also, he would hunt Blue a lot more than I could. I got older and moved on to other adventures, but on some occasions, my cousins would invite me to go with them.

On one of the occasions, my cousin came by my house one day and asked if he could come up one night and bring his young dogs to run a coon. We chose the night, and soon afterward, we were unloading the dogs. Now, the sport of coon hunting is to listen to the dogs run the coon, brag about whose dog is in the lead, run through the woods at night with the dogs, and celebrate when your dog trees first. However, this night was not about competition, it was a night to let the young dogs learn how to tree a coon. Quickly, the young dogs struck a coon: *Bahooooo*. The other dogs joined in, sounding like the good old days of the coon hunting adventures. Listening to good dogs running is like music to the ear of a coon hunter. Not long into the hunt, we heard a change in the dogs' sounds. *Yok Yok Yok.* The dogs had treed a coon. We were so excited for the young dogs and the experiences they were getting in treeing this coon. We did not want to hurt the coon. We only wanted the coon to jump out of the tree and onto the dogs for a little excitement, or strike up another race so the dogs could get more training. We worked our way to the tree. The dogs were under the tree, barking and looking up at the coon. The coon had climbed the tree and walked all the way out to the end of a limb. This was a small tree, so I thought I could take a long pole or stick and knock the coon out among the dogs. My cousin was standing about thirty feet from the tree that the coon was in, and the dogs were barking under the tree, looking up toward the coon. We all had the excitement of a coon hunt, but something was about to happen that I could not believe, and it had never happened before.

With a long pole, I punched the coon, and after a few knocks, the coon jumped out of the tree and hit the ground, running with the dogs right behind him. The coon was headed toward my cousin. I guess he thought he was a tree because all of a sudden, the coon ran up my cousin's leg, up to his shoulder and then on top of his head, and he jumped off the top of his head, hitting the ground and then running with the dogs two feet behind him. Thank goodness, my cousin had his cap on his head. All this happened without the coon missing a beat. I looked at my cousin and said, "That coon must have thought you were a tree!"

The dogs had another race to another tree. This time, the tree was so high we could not knock him out. So the coon lived to run another day. This was one hunt I will never forget. As I said, coon hunting was always an adventure, extremely exciting, and, in the case of the coon thinking my cousin was a tree, definitely full of the unexpected.

It Is Hard to Find Your Britches in the Dark in a Pine Tree Top

We lived in a house trailer in Auburn while attending college, like most everyone did in those days. Auburn was not known for tornadoes passing through like it was farther west over in Tuscaloosa. We would say maybe Auburn was safer than Tuscaloosa. We had lived there for a while and had the usual thunderstorms—but nothing like a tornado.

Everyone looked forward to spring break that year. Mostly, everyone would leave to go home or go on a vacation that week. Only a few students that had to work would stay in Auburn during spring break. My wife had to go home for spring break because her father had been sick and was recovering from heart problems. That left me at Auburn to work and fish with no studying. So I would put my days work in at the Auburn Vet School and then hurry to Lee County Lake to catch a few fish at the end of the day. On this particular day, I did not hear that any bad weather would be approaching that night or the next morning. I was young, and weather was the least of my concerns.

It was late that evening, and it was time to go to bed. As usual, I had just pulled my shirt and britches off, thrown them in the floor, and went to bed. Little did I know that I would need to find them quickly early in the following morning.

I was sleeping soundly early the next morning when at ten minutes after four, I was suddenly awakened by a loud roaring sound. It sounded like a train was coming into my bedroom. Instantly, I heard crashing sounds and windows being broken. Disoriented, I tried to figure out what was going on.

I saw the lightning, heard the thunder, and realized then that I was in a very bad storm. Then a big pine tree came crashing right into my bedroom. I had a big problem! With pine needles all around my bed, I immediately jumped off the bed onto the floor. There was another crash from a tree going through the kitchen window and one falling into the bathroom landing across the bathtub.

This was where the challenge of a lifetime came into play. I needed my britches! The power was out, it was pitch-black dark, and there was not even a flashlight to be found. I was crawling around on the floor, trying to find my britches in a pine tree top in the dark. I eventually found them and got them on, what a relief! I crawled through the pine tree top down the hall to the living room, where I was able to stand up for the first time. I went to the front door, opened it, and saw my neighbors going to their car. We could only see by the big lightning bolts, one right after another. It looked like a fireworks show. I yelled, "Where are ya'll going?" He said, "I don't know—anywhere but here!"

We all knew we had to get out of the mobile homes to be safe. I ran to their car and jumped in. We were going to try to make it to Haley Center for safety. We figured that it was a lot safer there than in a trailer. We were not prepared for what we were about to see: a power pole in the road, lines down, and house trailers upside down. It was a big disaster!

We made it through all that to get on Wire Road, which was the main road that passed by the vet school and leads straight to Auburn. Once we passed the vet school, it was not that bad. By the time we made it to Haley Center, the weather had calmed. It did not even seem like there had been a storm when we arrived.

At Haley Center, it seemed calm except for students talking about all the storm damage. We heard rumors that across Wire Road from where we lived in Barron's Trailer Court, the Gentilly Trailer Park had been wiped out. At daylight, we returned to our trailer park. Thank goodness for the pine trees that anchored my trailer down. We went over across the road to Gentilly Park and sure enough—the trailer park was totally destroyed. There was major damage throughout Auburn, but luckily, this was during spring break, or several people probably would have been killed. As far as I know, only a few injuries were treated at the infirmary and local hospital.

After the storm, we had our trailer repaired by the manufacturer. The company pulled it back to the plant and put it back together like new, replacing windows, repairing the metal frame, and putting on a new roof. Until our repairs were completed, we lived in a ten-by-forty trailer for three months. That was like living in a cracker box! We were so glad to get our trailer back that we celebrated when it arrived. There were some tough challenges going through school at Auburn, with difficult classes such as Organization and Administration of Health, Physical Education, and Recreation, Physiology, and Kinesiology. However, finding my britches in the dark in a pine tree top was definitely one of the hardest challenges I faced!

On the left, Harvey Robert "Papa" Woodard,
leading a Sacred Harp singing.

The Champion

Papa Woodard was a farmer, a logger, and a bee keeper who also worked in a sawmill in his younger days. He was one of the first school bus drivers in the county, purchasing his own school bus to transport children to and from school. He also was noted for making the best sorghum syrup in the community. His hobbies included singing and conducting at sacred harp singings, but everyone remembered him most for his checker playing.

Papa Woodard did not go to school a day in his life, or receive any sort of formal education. He taught himself how to read by reading the newspaper. I remember he was also very good at adding and subtracting numbers in his head. We called it "figuring" or "ciphering numbers" back in those days.

He attended sacred harp singings and learned how to read music. He became a leader at these singings and was well-known for his singing ability. He taught his children how to read the sacred harp shape notes. The whole family sounded outstanding when they all got together at reunions. I remember as a young man introducing my future wife to him. He asked her one question, "Can you play the 'Murillo's Lesson' song on the piano?" She played it for him, and he said, "You are all right girl!"

As a boy, I remember going to the woods to log with my dad and Papa Woodard. We did not have a power saw in those early days; instead, we used a crosscut saw to cut the logs. One man on each end pulling and pushing a six-foot saw was the way we got the job done. We used an ax to trim the limbs off the log. If you pulled a saw and used an ax all day long, no one had to rock you to sleep that night.

I remember how he loaded the smaller logs by standing the log on its end, walking under it, balancing it on his shoulder, and then tossing it into the truck. If it was a big log, the mules would snake the log up beside the truck. Two poles were placed on a slope from the truck to the ground. They would take a hand tool called a cant hook to roll the log up the poles into the truck. Papa also trained his mules to bring the logs to the truck themselves after someone hooked the logs up to them.

During his sawmill days, on one occasion, a rolling log went out of control, and Papa got his arm caught under this log, causing it to break in two places. When I asked my dad one day about the scars on Papa's arm, he told me about how the doctors had to wire the bones back together. Although today they would put pins in a break like that, this was how they had to fix compound fractures back then. Even though he sustained this injury and his bones were wired back together, his arm was still amazingly strong.

Papa was an amazing man in many ways, but he was mostly remembered for his leadership at sacred harp singings and his checker playing. Men would come from great distances to play Papa in checkers. As a boy growing up, I remember watching these games and having to be very quiet and not say a word during the game. I remember that he would not talk much while playing. He might say, "Is that your final move?" If you took your hand off the checker, that was considered your final move, and the move could not be changed. The game would usually end by him jumping your checkers with the words: "I cleaned your plow!"

My great uncles Pick, Leonard, Henry, Amos, and John David would all come to play Papa in checkers but could never beat him. Also, men from this county and other counties would come, but they would always lose. As I got older, I wanted to play Papa in checkers. We always played on the same board that he had used for many years. Some games might last an hour, but when I played Papa, it was the same outcome as when everyone else played him. When I would make a wrong move, he would jump my checkers, and I would hear the words: "I just cleaned your plow!" just the same as he said to everyone else.

I remember in my younger days I would cry every time I lost. He would not let me win even though I would cry. I would go home and say, "I am never going to play him again," but deep down, I had a major desire to beat him. As I got older, I would not cry, but I became more determined to learn how to beat him. Every day when we were not working, I would go up to Papa's place late in the evening to play checkers with him. Day after day, month after month, year after year, I would lose. I never won a game.

After many years of playing checkers, right before I graduated from high school, the day finally came that I beat him. He was so shocked. I was stunned and could not believe that I had actually done it. I could tell that it really hurt him because he had so much pride about his checker playing ability. I remember I could not wait to get home and tell everyone that I had finally beat Papa in a game of checkers. I felt a little sad for Papa because he had never lost a game that I knew of.

Later, I realized that I had gotten older, but Papa was getting old, and his mind may not have been as sharp as it was in his younger days. However, over the course of my entire childhood, he taught me a very valuable lesson through the simple game of checkers. I learned that if you have a desire to do something, if you try hard enough and long enough, you can accomplish that task. To achieve a goal, you have to have the desire, pay the price through time and hard work, and have the will to learn from others. I continued my checker playing for many years.

After attending Auburn University, I returned home and started teaching and coaching at Oneonta. It was a great opportunity. I used the simple game of checkers to teach my teams that there is a lot of difference between the type of player who wants to win a game versus the type of player who hates to lose. Give me the players or team that hate to lose every time. In my thirty-two years as a coach, I found that the team that hates to lose will always have the advantage.

One day, I had a little fun with the checker skills Papa had taught me. My wife was going to get her hair fixed in Oneonta, and I went with her. I had a couple of hours to kill, so I thought I would walk down to the farmers' market located behind Main Street. I immediately spotted some checker games going on at the lower end of the market. These games were being played by the old gentlemen of the county. So I walked over to the older gentlemen playing checkers and asked if I could play the best checker player there. They all pointed to a gentleman that I thought I recognized but could not recall his name. I could tell all the old men thought this game would be funny because a young man was just not going to win against the best player there. They all stopped their game and proceeded to watch. In their minds, young people were just not supposed to be any good at checkers because young people did not play the game that much.

After several people decided to gather around to watch, we finally got the game underway. The older gentleman thought he would clean my plow. It sure was a big surprise to him and all those watching when I won the game. He immediately asked, "What did you say your name was?" I told them my name, and one man said, "Did you say your granddaddy was named Rob Woodard?" I said, "Yes sir, it is." They said, "That explains it! We could never beat him in a game of checkers, he was the champion. He has taught you well!" The gentleman said, "Could I have another game?" We played the second game, and I won again. At this point, I thought I had better get out of there while my luck was still good. They wanted to play another game, but I told them my wife was about finished and I needed to go meet her.

On that day, I started another generation of playing checkers. One day, the older gentleman pulled up in my yard unexpectedly. I met him in the yard, and he said, "I thought if you have the time, I would like to try you in another game of checkers." I said, "Yes, that will be fun." That was the beginning of a long series of playing with him. The man came to my house on several occasions, as long as he could drive a car, to try his hand at beating me. Papa had taught me well, and I never let him beat me. I made a good friend with this man and respected him very much. I hope he had some enjoyment in his older days during the time we had together playing checkers.

When Papa died, I received his checkerboard. It hangs on the wall in my house as a reminder of the memories I have of playing checkers with him. The things you can learn from playing a simple game can be useful. These are good memories now that I cherish. I now have a better understanding of how valuable these days were playing checkers, and the things it taught me that I used in my everyday life. The memories that were left and the things he taught me in my young life are why I consider Papa "The Champion."

The author with a load of produce
on his farm in the 1970's.

The Farmers' Market

The first time I remember going to the farmers' market, I was probably about six years old. Of course, we did not sell out all the produce we carried, so we had to stay all night on the market to try to sell it. This would be the first of many nights in my life that I would spend sleeping on the tailgate or in the back of a truck. We would use hay or a rolled-up quilt that my mother had made to sleep on.

Dad started out planting an acre of squash and cucumbers in the spring, and he planted an acre every two weeks until he did not have time to plant any more. Along with the squash and cucumbers, he planted every kind of vegetable that he thought he could make any money on. That usually put us on the markets for the months of June, July, and August. A lot of days, Dad would leave with a load of produce to go to the market early in the morning, then go on to his job at General Steel Tank that evening. After spending all morning on the farmers market, then putting in eight hours of welding at General Steel, he would typically get home around 2:00 am.

Dad would usually take his month of vacation time in July so that he could haul the largest part of produce to the market. When I turned about fourteen years old, Dad started letting me have my own patches of vegetables. My first time to drive home from the market was when I was only fourteen. I did not have my license yet. I was on the market when a neighbor had a heart attack while we were down there. The other neighbor wanted me to drive his truck home, and I did. It was about three o'clock in the morning, so I did not meet very many cars. By the time I was fifteen and got my permit to drive, I was driving the load of produce to the market, and mother would go with me on these trips. By the time I was sixteen, I was going by myself.

When I was seventeen, we planted every inch of ground in produce. Also, we rented our neighbor's farm and planted patches of produce on it as well. I remember sleeping on the tailgate of the truck on the market for thirty nights in a row that summer. As soon as I would get home in the mornings, another load was loaded on the truck and back I would go to the market. The reason you wanted to be on the tailgate is because you did not want to miss a buyer. Buyers walked the market all night long looking for a bargain. Buyers could find a deal especially when a farmer was tired and was ready to go home.

Dad would always give me a spot of ground that I could plant for my own, but of course, it was grown up in bushes. So I would clear it, plant it in peas, and make good money. The next year, he would plant it in corn and give me another patch to clear up and plant for the next year. I did clear up a lot of land doing this! I remember at age seventeen, I had a plan to get rich in one year, or so I thought. Along with all the other vegetable patches, I decided I was going to plant two acres of pole beans. My cousin helped me, and we cut bean sticks all winter and spring in our spare time. We had a big pile of bean sticks. When spring came, I planted these Kentucky Wonder pole beans really early. We start sticking these beans and found out right quick we did not have enough sticks to stick the two acres. We did go back and cut enough to finish the job before the bean runners got too long on the beans.

Having two acres of pole beans is a lot of work because you not only have to stick them, but you also have to help the runners get started up the stick every day. I had to plow, hoe, and keep the row and the middles clean. I also had to dust the beans with Sevin Dust to keep the bugs and beetles off the beans. Those beans really made good that year. The first picking produced about twenty-five bushels.

Picking and washing beans and getting them in the bushel baskets certainty took a lot of work, but I had plenty of good help. I pulled into the market and sold the beans for six dollars a bushel! I was a very happy boy. About five days later, we picked almost a hundred bushels of pole beans off this patch. It took us all day, and I got to the market late, around nine that night. When I pulled onto the market I had a couple of buyers walk up to my truck. They said, "How much for the beans?" I was feeling very confident that I would get six dollars a bushel again for all the beans, so I said, "Six dollars." They said they would give me five dollars a bushel—and I said no.

When buyers came again at five the next morning, I felt confident that I would get my price of six dollars a bushel. I did sell four or five bushels at six dollars, just enough to make me think I was going to be able to sell them all at that price. The man that had bought the previous load at six dollars walked by and offered me five and a quarter for the beans and said he would take them all. Again, I said no because I was trying to hold out to get six dollars a bushel. It was not thirty minutes later that two or three truck loads of pole beans pulled in across from me from a county south of us. I saw that they started selling beans very quickly. I walked over and asked them how much they were getting for their beans. They said four dollars a bushel. Being young, and thinking I had it all under control, I walked down to the man that made me the offer on the beans at five and a quarter and told him he could have them. He said, "Sorry, I have already bought." I thought I would be smart and let them sell all their beans first and then I would get my price.

About seven o'clock the next morning, that idea went down the drain when about ten new loads of beans came pulling into the market within an hour. I now saw that they were asking $2.50 and $3.00 a bushel. The market price had dropped that fast. I was so mad that I said I would not take that for my beans! I would feed them to the hogs! Well, I sat there all day, all night, and all the next day, selling only a few more bushels. Finally, I begged a man to take the remaining of them for two dollars a bushel.

After several days on the market, this was one lesson that I will never forget! I did continue to pick my beans and sold most of them for two and three dollars a bushel that year. I made a little money on my beans, but my dream of getting rich; well, let's just say that didn't happen.

On another occasion, after I was married, my decisions on the market paid off. We put out two acres of tomatoes one year really early. We had the first Blount County tomatoes and got three dollars a basket for them, which was good. Three dollars a basket was a lot of money for a basket of tomatoes back then. A buyer on the market bought them from us because he could advertise he had the first Blount County tomatoes. The average price was about two dollars back then. The price of tomatoes usually dropped after the Fourth of July, and you would be lucky to get a dollar per basket.

The next year we planted three acres of tomatoes. We set them out very early, and by mid-May, they were loaded with little tomatoes, and the vines were full of blooms. That year, the worst hail storm came that I can ever remember. The rain and hail beat the vines into the ground, and it shredded the leaves, blooms, and little tomatoes off the stems. When I walked out there after the storm, I did not know if the tomatoes would put back out and make anything, but I plowed them and put the fertilizer to them. The tomatoes put back out with twice as many vines, but I knew it was going to make the tomatoes be late and come in after the Fourth of July, which meant lower prices. However, the first load made it by the Fourth of July, and I got two dollars a basket for them. The second picking was a big one, loading the truck down. That tomato patch made the most tomatoes I had ever seen. The ground and vines were covered in tomatoes. When I got to the market though, there were tomatoes everywhere. I stayed down there for two days, trying to sell that load of tomatoes. Finally, I sold out for about fifty cents a basket.

I came home and told everyone that we would pick all the ripe tomatoes all the way down to the big green ones, if they had just a little pink on them. I planned to store them in my cool basement and hold them as long as I could. Every day, we would pick the pink ones and add to the pile and go throw the bad ones away, which were not that many. The cool basement was the perfect place for storing vegetables and fruit (we once stored over a hundred bushels of sweet potatoes over the winter, and they kept very well). We had my basement full of tomatoes. After about ten days, I loaded up the truck and headed to the market. I was surprised when I pulled up on the market, and there were not many tomatoes. I was afraid to ask two dollars a basket, but I did. It was not long before I sold out and was on my way home for another load. A lot of farmers had stopped picking because the tomatoes had gotten too cheap to haul and just left them in the field. The sun was so hot for ten days that it burned a lot of tomatoes up in the field, but we had all our tomatoes in cool storage. We got around two dollars a basket for the rest of our tomatoes and were able to turn two disasters, the hail storm and the flooded market, into a good profit off that tomato patch. That patch made so many tomatoes I did not think we would ever get all of them picked. I believe the hail storm made them produce twice as much and the fact that we picked all of them as soon as they turned pink made for a record crop.

There were things you had too learn to beware of on the market. After dark, you did not get too far away from the farmers' row of trucks. There had been farmers robbed, stabbed, and I knew of one person being killed. So, it was very dangerous at night on the market. However, to make money selling produce, you had to accept that the market could be a little dangerous. You had to really hustle, and sometimes, that meant working twenty-four hours a day.

After I was married, my wife and I had a load of cantaloupes on the Birmingham market. One night, a man called Red, who had bought a lot of produce from me over the years, asked me to drive a load of produce to the Atlanta market for him and bring back a load of tomatoes. I knew him well, so I said yes. I only had a few cantaloupes left on the truck. He told me that if I would drive a load of produce to Atlanta, he would buy my cantaloupes and pay me fifty dollars to drive to Atlanta and back. I said okay.

It was about twelve o'clock that night by the time we got loaded and left for Atlanta. I figured we would be back by daylight with an extra fifty dollars. I had been up several nights in a row and was tired. My wife was with me, and she was also very tired, but we needed the extra money. About halfway to Atlanta, after dozing off to sleep, she woke up and saw me headed straight for the corner of a bridge. She yelled at me to wake me up just in time for me to get the truck back on the road. It scared us both so much that neither one of us got sleepy the rest of the night! She stayed awake to make sure that I did not go to sleep again. We made several of these trips over the summer for the man. Most of them were at night, and we made fifty dollars while everyone else was sleeping, plus it was a way to sell our produce to Red. Red was a produce broker, and his warehouse on the market was the place where several buyers for grocery stores came to buy produce.

When school let out in the summer, I would go to Cordell, Georgia, to buy loads of cantaloupes to resell back home before we had ripe ones in our patch to haul. I would leave in time to get to Cordell by nine o'clock at night. It was a good six-hour drive, especially loaded with produce. I would load the truck by ten and be back by daylight the next morning. Then my wife would take them to Huntsville and sell them at a stand we had rented and paid for. The best trip we made was on one occasion when I bought them for a dime a piece and she sold them for a dollar each. I brought back nine hundred cantaloupes. I even had them stacked in the cab with me! We took the clear profit and went on our summer vacation.

I hauled several loads of cantaloupes from Cordell over the years. There was about a two-week period of time that you could catch the Cordell market flooded, and that was when the cantaloupes were cheap. This was usually about two weeks right before the Fourth of July. On one of these trips the next year, we drove two trucks to Cordell during this time period when their markets were flooded with cantaloupes. When we got back, I took one truck to Birmingham to sell, and my wife and her sister took the other truck to Huntsville. They sold the entire load in two hours and were back home by lunch! Of course, it took me all day to sell my load and for less than they sold their load. We all wanted to take our money and go to Opryland Park for our vacation before we had to start working very hard when all our produce would get ripe.

The next morning, we went to Tennessee, and when we pulled into the motel where we were going to spend the night, my sister-in-law put her purse on top of the car when she got out and was getting children and bags out. She got her purse, but somehow, her billfold with all her money fell out into the parking lot, and we did not notice it. We walked to a nearby restaurant to eat lunch, and as we were getting ready to pay, she could not find her billfold. She had about six hundred dollars in the billfold. I paid for all our lunches, and we walked back to the motel and looked all around the car, inside the car, everywhere, but we could not find the billfold. We were all just sick because that was a lot of money to lose. My brother-in-law decided to go inside the motel to see if someone found it, and when he came back out he told us the manager had it because someone turned it into him with all the money still inside. We all thanked the Lord and were very grateful! My brother-in-law was given the name of the person that found it, and he called him to thank him and offer him a reward, but the man said no and he would only hope that someone would be kind enough to return the favor if that had happened to him. He thanked the man several times, and we all felt so blessed and felt like God was watching over us that day. We knew the golden rule, "Do unto others as you would have them do unto you" was in place that day.

The Crosstie Put
My Lights Out

In my early twenties, my father-in-law sold some property in Oneonta that was covered in big pine trees. He had built a fence many years before around the property using railroad crossties. When he sold this property, he reserved the right to cut the pines for logs and remove the crossties that held the fence up going around the property line. After the pines were removed, he made me an offer. If I did all the work of removing all the crossties, we would divide them so that I could get two and he would get one. I would haul his load of twenty-five and deliver them to his house, and I would bring two loads of twenty-five to my house.

I had a Ford 2000 tractor that I used to snake the crossties to the trailer that I was hauling them on. Snaking them means you tie a chain to one end of the big railroad crosstie and pull it behind the tractor to the trailer. (This was long before any farmers in this area had a tractor with a front-end loader.) To pull the crossties out of the ground, I used a chain that was tied to a drawbar, which went across my three-point hitch. All I had to do was back the drawbar up against a crosstie, wrap the chain around the crosstie twice, and tie it at the very bottom of the crosstie next to the ground. I would then get back on the tractor, back up and pull forward to shake the crosstie loose from the ground, and use the hydraulic lift to pick it up off the ground. Once the upright crosstie was out of its hole in the ground, I would back up my tractor to lay the crosstie flat on the ground. I would use the hydraulic lift to pick up the end with the chain around it about a foot and half off the ground. I would then head to the trailer snaking the crosstie, with a chain on one end of the crosstie tied to my drawbar and the other end dragging along the ground.

I picked out a path that was clear of stumps and brush to travel back and forth. I would usually take the same path. After getting all the ones close to the truck, I had to start traveling a longer distance to each crosstie across the forty acres, with the farthest distance being about a quarter of a mile. Finally, I made a path over a pine stump, which was cut about a foot off the ground. In this area, the stumps were just too thick for me to find a path to go between. I did not think anything about it because I had snaked some other crossties over some other stumps. All I had to do was pick my lift up a little higher for the crosstie to clear the stumps.

I hauled crossties for several days and was almost finished. I had half of a load on the trailer, and it was mid-afternoon. I was snaking this crosstie down the path that I had already traveled down several times when I let my concentration down and was thinking of something else. Since I had been over this path several times, I was moving pretty fast. As usual, I was in a hurry and was working at full speed. All of a sudden, the end of the crosstie closest to the tractor hit a pine stump. The crosstie did not bounce off the stump. Instead, the crosstie hit the pine stump solidly, causing the other end of the crosstie to flip completely over and hit me and the tractor seat. Thank goodness I was leaning forward in the seat. However, I immediately was knocked out. God either turned the tractor off, or God took my hand and cut it off because I don't remember doing it myself. However, I do remember seeing stars.

When I woke up, the tractor was stopped still, the engine was shut off, and the crosstie was lying on the back of the tractor seat and on my right shoulder, right above my shoulder blade with the end on my head. As I woke up, I realized that my shoulder was hurting badly, as was my head. I got off the tractor and walked to the truck thinking I would be okay. I was three miles from the Oneonta Hospital but thinking I was okay, I drove fifteen miles home.

As I walked in the house, I sat down in the first chair by the door and told my wife that I got hurt and my head still hurt really badly. She checked my head and found a big knot with blood and told me I was talking funny. She immediately put me in a car and took me to a hospital in Birmingham. On the way to Birmingham, I realized how badly I might be hurt. I also could not remember how I got to the point of riding down the road to Birmingham. I do not ever remember, even to this day, driving home from Oneonta.

When we arrived at the emergency room, the doctors told my wife that I had a bad concussion and a knot about the size of a pancake on my head. He told her he would need to do some tests on my head, and he also said he would be doing an X-ray on my shoulder because I had a blue place the size of the crosstie on my shoulder. He thought it was possibly broken. When the doctor came back to the room, he said he found no blood clots. He joked with my wife and said I had a hard head. Then he told us that the shoulder was not broken, but he could see on the bones an imprint of the crosstie. He then said that I had the hardest bones of any person he had ever seen and that I had a bad concussion and some swelling on my brain. I was held in the hospital in intensive care for several days and then moved to a regular room for a few more days. For the first day in the intensive care unit, they would not let me go to sleep. Every twenty or thirty minutes, the nurse would come in and shine a light in my eyes to check for any changes. Once I moved out to a regular room, I was glad to be able to get some rest.

After leaving the hospital, I had an appointment in five days to go back to this doctor for a checkup, and it turned out fine. After this incident, he became my doctor until he retired. He always laughed and joked with me every time he saw me about my hard head and the crosstie. He said that hard of a hit on the head should have killed me. I know I had help from God with the turning off of the tractor, driving home, and being okay. Thankfully, the tractor seat and my shoulder took most of the force from the crosstie, and if I had not been leaning forward, the crosstie would have hit my head first, and I probably would have been killed. The day the crosstie put my lights out, God was watching over me and had his hand on the situation in every way.

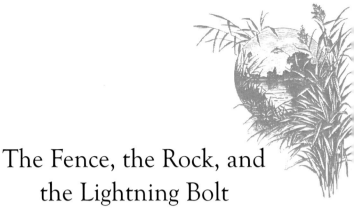

The Fence, the Rock, and
the Lightning Bolt

Building fences is hard work, but a necessity on a cattle farm. Besides getting cut up by the wire, there are many other ways that you can get hurt. Driving steel posts by hand is a tough job, but digging postholes with a set of hand-held posthole diggers is even tougher, especially when you hit rocks.

My father-in-law decided one day that he wanted me to help him build a fence on the property line for two miles around the back side of the farm. Most of the fence would be through the woods up a steep mountain, and through lime rock territory which held many rattlesnakes. This meant driving steel posts through cracks and crevices in lime rocks, and digging the corners through rock using a steel bar and hand-held posthole diggers. We could not access this property with the tractor, so all the post and wire had to be carried in on foot. Building this fence was some of the hardest work I have ever done, and I almost got killed doing it. One thing's for sure, I learned a lot about determination and strong will on this fence building project.

My father-in-law wanted a good fence that was built tight, straight, and on the property line. That was a challenge within itself. Building a good fence is hard on level ground, but it is especially hard going up and down steep mountains and through rocks. The fence project was going as well as it could go, until we found out the fence was going to cross right over a six-foot-high rock. I suggested we could build the fence over the top of the rock. My father-in-law said, "No." So I said, "We could move over a little and build the fence around the rock." Again, my father-in-law said, "No, I don't like that. I want it on the line." So I said, "Well, what are you going to do?" He said, "We are going to move the rock and build the fence straight and on the line."

My first thought was that we couldn't do that because that rock was too big. We could not get a tractor up there on the mountain to move the rock, which was six feet tall, six feet wide, ten feet long, and deep in the ground. I asked how he planned to move a rock of that size without a tractor. He said, "We will move the rock one piece at a time with a sledge hammer, chisel, wedge, and iron bar."

Four hours later, the rock was cut down to ground level. We accomplished this by placing a wedge in the cracks of the rock and driving the wedge in with a sledge hammer until we cracked it. Then we would take the iron bar and long poles and use them as a lever to pry the rock off piece by piece.

After we removed the rock, we continued on building the fence, which is still there today, built straight, tight, and crosses right over where the rock used to be. That was one of the hardest tasks I have ever attempted. Although I was not sure if we could do it, we were able to finish the job. However, before the fence was completed, I would experience another day that I would never forget.

We had worked on the fence all morning and thought we might finish the fence on that day. A little storm came up around lunchtime, so we went to the house for lunch. Around one o' clock, we returned to work on the fence. It was still thundering off in the distance. We were about to finish up the fence when the lightning started to get a little closer. At that time, I was not too afraid because the lightning was off at a distance. My father-in-law was not afraid of lightning at all, and as a matter of fact, I don't think he was afraid of anything. We were tying the wire to a big oak tree where three fences came together from three different directions. I had stretched the last strand of wire, and my father-in-law was pulling on the fence stretchers because he wanted it tighter. I had just completed tying the wire around the tree, so I decided to cut the wire off the remaining roll. Just as I cut the wire and my father-in-law turned loose of the wire stretchers, I heard a tingling sound in the wire. I thought, what *was that sound!* But then, *kaboom*, it was lightning! When you hear the electricity before you see it, you know you are too close.

I heard the thunder and saw the lightning at the same time, and then the bark flew from the big oak tree. The lightning bolt knocked the bark from the tree and knocked a hole in the ground right in front of me! I felt the hair on my body fly up from my skin. I jumped very high and backward all at one time! I was scared. Our cattle dog named Big Boy started yelling like he had been hit. He started running toward our trailer that was hooked to the back of the tractor. Big Boy went right up under that trailer, and I did the same! I got up under the trailer with Big Boy for safety. I told my father-in-law that we had better go to the house. My father-in-law said, "Lightning doesn't strike twice in the same spot." About the time he said it, *kaboom*, it proved him wrong.

I figured if Big Boy felt safe enough to stay under the trailer, I should do the same. My father-in-law just kept on working on the fence like he had no fear. I guess his experience of serving our country in World War II had made him not to be afraid of anything. He had told me about the time he was at Iwo Jima when the USA made the landing. He said the orders were to take that mountain no matter what. He talked about soldiers falling on both sides of him and walking on dead bodies as he and other soldiers continued on toward the mountain, fighting and firing his rifle as he went. When it was over, they had taken the mountain and raised the American flag. That one sentence he said always made me admire him for what he did for our country. I guess, after going through all that in the war, it made lightning seem not all that bad. He lived to be ninety and was never afraid of lightning. We were fortunate that day that both of us had just turned loose of the wire and the stretcher when the lightning bolt hit, or we both would have been killed.

The fence still had to be completed, so after a while, we both continued on working. Although we had hoped to be able to finish that day, it still took a few more days work. The total project was a major undertaking that required a lot of hard work and took a couple of months to complete. The fence is still there today, and it is built straight, tight, and well. It took lots of blood, sweat, and determination to finish the fence. We could have lost our lives from the lightning, but we got the job done.

The lessons I learned from this fence-building project were that you might not think you can do something, but you can, if you are determined enough. You never know what you can do until you try. If you are determined enough, you just might be able to do it, just like we moved the rock. I will never forget that day the lightning hit the fence and tree and made my hair rise up on my arms. Hearing the electricity tingling in the wire before I heard the lightning bolt was also something that I hope I never hear again. I will also not forget how Big Boy ran under the trailer yelling and how I followed right behind him and crawling up under the trailer with him, but my father-in-law just kept right on working like he was not afraid. The rock was moved, the fence was built, and we survived the lightning bolts. However on that day, I really learned to respect lightning. Thank God for allowing us to survive the lightning bolts and for watching over us on many other dangerous occasions and allowing us another day on this earth.

This plow, called a "middle buster" was used
many times on our farm to plow up potatoes.

Learn by Doing

The best way to learn something is by doing it. The more times you do it, the better you will get at it. As they say, practice makes perfect.

In order to learn a skill and master it well, you have to want to learn it. When you want and seek out knowledge, you will learn far more than if those things are simply forced upon you.

My dad was a believer in the method of "learn by doing." This is one lesson he taught me from a very young age. He wanted me to learn things for myself and stand on my own two feet. He was a master teacher of farming skills because he had learned them through many years of experience. He was also a master welder and a class-one welder of aluminum fuel tanks. Although his welding skills were self-taught, he became very good at it. Eventually, he became the top welder at General Steel Tank.

"Learning by doing" was the method he used to teach us many things. A good example would be when he taught us to swim. He put me on a rock out in the

Robert Earl Woodard

middle of the river and told me to jump in and swim to him. I trusted him so much I jumped in and hit the water, paddling. It is amazing how quickly you can learn to swim when you think you are about to go under the water. Later in life, when I taught freshman swimming at Auburn, I realized this may not have been the best method of teaching beginners, but it was very effective. Dad said if he had not taught my brother and me to swim, he knew we would not have made it. Most likely because we would be on the river one day by ourselves without him, and we had to know how to swim to take care of ourselves. He was so right.

We watched him, and we learned how to do all kinds of things because we never knew when he would say, "Now, I want you to do this." If I didn't know how to do something on the farm, I had to learn quickly. His method was the method of "learn by doing" because he expected me to get the job done with no excuses. Many things you have to learn in life are a lot like plowing a mule. You can have someone standing there telling you how to plow for hours and hours, but the best way to learn is just to take the plow by the handles and the plow lines in your hand and start plowing. You learn how to control the plow with a little pressure on the handles, learn how to control the mule with your voice, and learn how to do a better job with practice and experience.

Just like learning to plow a mule, that was how I learned to drive a tractor and a truck. The day we got our very first tractor on the farm, I was on it that day, learning how to drive it. The saying "learn by doing" comes down to about everything you try in life, including fishing, hunting, and your job. Farming is a continual learning process, as things are always changing. Teaching is also a job where something new comes along every day. So in my jobs, I have had to learn the new ways, all of which were learned by doing.

Learning technology is a new skill I have had to acquire. When computers and cell phones first came out, I was not interested in them. I had difficulty learning because I did not think I would ever need to use them. However, I soon developed an interest, and before I knew it, I was fairly good at it. I have not learned everything there is to know about new technologies, but I've learned enough to do what I need to keep up with the fast pace of the changing world. I found out to move ahead and keep up in the changing world; I needed to learn these skills. The same principles that applied to learning technology in more recent years applied to plowing the mule when I was a boy. You have to put your mind to it and learn by doing.

I did not have typing class in school. However, I have been able to teach myself, and I typed this book. I have learned a lot while writing it, just as I have learned many things throughout my life. The key has always been having the desire to learn new skills, broaden your horizons, and be willing to change to meet the challenges of a fast-moving world.

I would like to conclude this short story with a few more old sayings that have been passed down in my family through the generations. I believe that "anything worth doing is worth doing right" and that "a stitch in time saves nine." I believe that you should always "do your best because that's all a mule can do." "Never give up on anything you start. Always finish it." I believe that you should "stand up for what is right, and you will be all right." I believe that "your word is the most important thing you have. It is worth more than money." These sayings were passed down by people of wisdom who had lived a full life and had learned by living it. These sayings will take you a long way toward being successful in life.

There Are Just Some Days You Don't Forget

Everyone has certain days in their life which stand out in their mind, sometimes many years after the events have occurred. Many of the stories presented throughout this book are from days in my life that always stand out in my mind when I think back over the years. The following short stories are a few more days that I will never forget.

The Day the Mule Ran Away

I always remember those long, hot days plowing mules while growing up on the farm. I can remember the bad, like the gnats trying to bite me on those hot and humid days, as well as the good, like the tomato sandwiches with sweet tea at lunch and how delicious that simple meal was during a hard day's work. After lunch, we would get a fresh mule and go back to plowing until sundown when it was time to take the mule to the barn for feed and water. Both the mule and I would need a good dinner and some rest so that we would be ready for the next day.

Years later, as a school teacher, I would wonder if there were any boys left with the strength and endurance to follow a mule from sunup to sundown. There were a few children that I thought needed that lesson so they could learn to appreciate what they had. Although each generation has it a little easier, I wonder sometimes if we have made life too convenient for our children in this modern world.

One day on our farm, we had a mule that refused to plow, which resulted in a very exciting day on our farm that I will always remember. My dad thought we needed to get a new mule on the farm to add to the ones we already had. He thought that by swapping out for a fresh mule in the middle of the day, we would be able to plow more in a day. One day, I was plowing one of our good mules when I saw Dad coming up the edge of the field with a new mule. It was a good-looking mule and appeared to have a lot of potential. At that time, I had never plowed a mule that was not a proven reliable plowing mule. However, that was about to change.

The man who sold the mule had said he was broken to plow. We hooked him up to the scratcher gang plows. Dad had plowed with him a little and thought that he was okay. After a short while, Dad passed him off to me. I could tell immediately that I did not like him as well as the mules that I was used to. The mule was nervous and not smooth to plow like our other mules. After three or four rounds, he seemed to be settling down, and I thought everything would be okay. However, just as I started to think this, the mule broke away and started running across the field towards the woods!

There I was out in the middle of the field when this mule decided to head across the rows of corn toward the woods, with me desperately trying to stop the mule. At the same time, I was struggling to hold the plow up so that it would not plow up the corn as the mule ran across the field. Although the mule probably thought he would make his escape, he did not know that Dad would be waiting for him when he got to the shade at the edge of the woods.

Both Dad and I were very upset with the mule. Obviously, Dad was frustrated because he thought that he had bought a mule that was broken to plow. After Dad had a little "attitude adjustment session" with the mule, he put the mule to a turning plow. After an hour with the turning plow, Dad thought he would be ready to again try to plow corn with the scratcher gang plow. As soon as he tried this, though, the mule sulled and would not walk. Dad tried to get him to go, and when he tapped him with the plow line, the mule broke into a run. Dad struggled to stop him and succeeded in stopping him for a moment—only for the mule to break into another run. Dad just let him go to the end of the field and said, "This mule just won't plow, and we don't need this mule! We don't have the time to waste fooling with this crazy mule because we have work to do."

Dad unhooked the mule, led him straight to the truck, loaded him up, and drove him back to the man who had sold Dad the mule. I learned on this day that some mules just won't plow!

Friends and Neighbors

I remember my dad hiring a neighbor, who was one of my mother's dearest friends, to help us work in the fields. He paid her five dollars a day for hoeing in the fields, which was what a person received per day in those days for hoeing or plowing. As a boy growing up, I thought a lot of this lady. She was always very sweet and kind to me and full of wisdom.

Many years later, I would teach school with her granddaughter, and we would become very close friends. Obviously, I had no way of knowing back when I was a boy that we would become such close friends many years later. As we made our journey down through the years teaching school, we made many memories and talked about many old memories from the days of working in the fields. She helped me in many ways in school and taught both of my children in high school.

Sometimes in life, things come full circle, like friends and neighbors. The granddaughter of one of my mother's closest friends would wind up becoming one of my closest friends decades later. They worked in the fields together, and we worked in the classrooms together. It is friends and neighbors like these that make work and life enjoyable.

Picking Peppers

I will never forget the memories of getting up on Saturday mornings at daylight and having to pick peppers after having played in a football game the night before. Usually, I did not get in the bed until twelve or one after the game.

The next morning, I was usually so sore I could barely move. I guess picking peppers was a good way to work the stiff muscles out because by nine o'clock, I could move well. Dad, Mother, and I would pick a ton of pepper every Saturday morning during the fall.

Once we had them all picked, we would haul them to Albertville and receive $220 for the ton of peppers. We did this every Saturday morning until a frost. It was hard work, but we made good money. In addition to making some good money, it helped work all my sore muscles out so that I was ready for football practice on Monday.

Hauling Watermelons

I had hauled many watermelons by the time I was sixteen. One fall, a neighbor had a big watermelon patch of jubilee melons, averaging about fifty pounds each. He came up to the house one day and asked me if I would help him pick and load the melons. He also asked if I could get a friend to help me. He said he would pay us a dollar an hour, so I told him I would get a friend to help me. He said he would pick us up at five the next morning. I had my friend ready to go and was standing on the road the next morning waiting on him.

He picked us up, and we arrived at the field around five thirty. We saw two eighteen-wheeler trucks, a ton truck, a tractor with a long trailer behind it, and a pickup truck that were all empty. The man drove the tractor with the trailer through the field, and we loaded the melons on the long trailer. When the trailer was full, we unloaded the bigger melons on the eighteen-wheeler and the smaller melons on the ton truck. Some of the largest melons weighed seventy-five to eighty pounds, and the smaller melons were around thirty to forty pounds. Since I could drive the tractor, the man said he would go get our lunch. He brought us back a hamburger and a Coke. In those days, a burger and Coke were under two dollars. We stopped just long enough to eat, and then it was right back to work picking up those big melons.

My friend and I were in good shape, and we considered ourselves to be very tough. We had so much pride—we certainly were not going to let the man know we were getting tired late in the afternoon. About the time we loaded the last eighteen-wheeler truck with all the melons it would hold, we were very tired. The sun was going down, and we had to finish loading the ton truck and the pickup before dark. It was almost dark when we thought we were through. The man said we needed to go back and load the long trailer behind the tractor that we had used all day. When we got the trailer behind the tractor loaded, it was flat dark. Then he decided to load some melons on the pickup that he was driving to the patch. We loaded it after dark by using the head lights on the other truck to see.

My friend and I were so glad when we got that last melon loaded and were able to sit down on the seat of the truck. We both felt like we had done a day's work and could not pick up another melon. We did not know how many melons we loaded that day—but it was a lot! The man carried us home and let us out on the road near my house around nine-thirty. He gave us ten dollars each and said, "I took out money for y'alls lunch." We were taught to be respectful to adults, so we did not say a thing.

After the man pulled off, my friend said, "I will never haul another melon for that man." I also felt the same way and never worked for him again.

Lots of Cantaloupes and Two Tough Ladies

I will never forget the time we contracted to sell our cantaloupes to a buyer out of Tennessee. Since Dad was working day shift on his job in Birmingham at that time, it was left up to Mother and me to pick them. I went to my best friend's house to ask if he and his mom could help us pick cantaloupes on that day. I had helped them on many days picking produce, so they were good with helping us. That was how neighbors helped each other back then.

My friend and I would carry all the cantaloupes to the truck and wagon so that our moms could pick them up and put them in bushel baskets. As soon as our moms filled one bushel basket, we had an empty basket set in front of them. Occasionally, we would pick up cantaloupes and help them fill their basket if they did not have it full when we returned. I know one thing—we really worked hard carrying those cantaloupes to the truck and wagon parked at the edge of the field. We could not drive through the field because we would mash and destroy too many cantaloupes. So we had to carry them by hand, usually up on top of our shoulders, in a bushel basket to the wagon and truck.

I know my friend and I worked hard on that day, but our mothers outworked us. I have never seen two women pick up over two hundred bushels of cantaloupes in one day. It would take ten to twelve cantaloupes to make one bushel, depending on the size of the cantaloupe. I doubt many other women would be able to do that strenuous type of work. Our mothers were used to this type of work, which they had done all their lives. Working that hard every day had made them very strong ladies.

Late that afternoon, the man from Tennessee was waiting at our house to load the cantaloupes he had purchased. We loaded him two hundred bushels of good cantaloupes for two dollars a bushel. We had another twenty or so bushels of smaller and cull cantaloupes that we put on the side of the road and sold for a dollar a dozen. We sold most of them, and the hogs got the rest after a few days. In two days, we had more cantaloupes to pick, and the man from Tennessee bought the entire patch. Thanks to this, we did not have to haul any to the market that year, which was great. As I remember, that cantaloupe patch made lots of good cantaloupes. However, the main thing I remember is just how hard our mothers worked getting those cantaloupes so that we could sell them to the man from Tennessee.

Hay Hauling

Hauling square bales of hay can be a very hard job. Putting them up in a barn loft can make it even harder. I've hauled many square bales of hay in my time. When I was younger, my father-in-law would usually put up six to eight thousand bales a year. We had many hired hands to go home, saying that it was too hard of work. Even worse, if you told them you were going to be hauling hay all day and putting it in a barn loft, they would not even come or show up.

The summer before my senior year of high school, my future father-in-law was going to bale twenty-four acres of hay. He wanted my cousin and me to haul it in for him. He would pay us a dollar an hour, the usual pay for hauling hay during that time. I don't know why we thought we could haul all this hay in by ourselves. We did not realize that from those twenty-four acres, it was going to produce nearly two thousand bales of hay. My future father-in-law could not even bale it all in one day. He did bale over fourteen hundred that day while we hauled the hay to the barn and put it in the barn loft.

My cousin and I started hauling around ten o'clock that morning. By ourselves, we hauled and put 1,188 bales in the barn loft the first day. We put the last bale up in the barn that evening when it was so dark we could barely see. That had never been done before on that farm, nor has it ever been done since. I imagine that record will stand forever, since these days we do round bales.

Too Much Hay

One summer, I decided to purchase a trailer truck load of square bales. This hay had been baled and loaded with an accumulator and then loaded onto an eighteen-wheeler. Since this hay had been intended to be handled by equipment, the bales were packed very tightly. Most of them weighed about seventy-five pounds. I had bought 680 bales, which made a full load.

I had planned to unload the truck on a Saturday morning with my son. It was July, so it was a very hot day.

When we started unloading this truck, it was not too bad. However, the farther back into the truck we went, the farther we had to carry the bales by hand. Also, since the trailer was too tall to back into the barn, once we had the bales off the trailer, we had to carry them and stack them in the back of the barn.

This started getting very tiring, carrying those seventy-five-pound bales from one end of the trailer to the other, throwing them off, and then carrying them to stack them in the back of the barn. Before we finished, I simply gave out of strength. I realized at almost fifty years old, I could not haul hay like I could when I was in high school. I told my son if he could finish, go ahead.

I got my second wind and helped him on the last few bales to finish the job. After we finished, my son told me to write myself a note and put it on the refrigerator door to never do that again! I listened, and I have never again purchased an entire tractor trailer load of square bales for us to unload by hand. That started a saying in our family that if you didn't want to do something again because you found a better way, you would write a note to yourself and put it on the refrigerator door. This has been a joke in our family ever since that day. I suppose that was just one more case of "learn by doing."

Days to Remember:
Accomplishments and Milestones

Looking back, many days from my life that stick out in my mind are from days of very hard work that I, my family, and my friends have done together during my life.

However, some of the days that I remember most weren't days that involved work on the farm but were instead days of reaching accomplishments or passing milestones in my life, or in the lives of my family.

I will always remember the day my wife and I got married. That was a very special day, and we've been going strong every since. I will always remember the day we graduated from Auburn University. We were so proud to have achieved this goal and were excited to start our new careers. I remember the day both of my children were born. Their days in school, watching them grow up was very rewarding for us. Both received many awards and recognition during their high school and college years, for both academics and music. Both were valedictorian, and received full scholarships. It makes me very proud of their accomplishments. They used the work ethic our family has used for years on the farm and used it toward their education and earning a scholarship.

Both received scholarships from several major universities. My daughter chose the University of Alabama, accepting the top scholarship to the school of music. My son chose Auburn University, receiving the top presidential academic scholarship to the school of business. I was very proud of them for graduating with honors from these universities. They both have good jobs, and I am proud that they use the same work ethic that was used on the farm by my grandparents, my parents, and my wife and me. Most importantly, I am proud they carry on the tradition of hard work that has been passed down in my family, earning their way in life.

The author with a nine point buck
that he killed by stalk hunting.

The Big Buck

In my young adult life, I became determined to be a good deer hunter. My goal was to hunt the biggest bucks. First of all, you have to know if a big buck is using the area and then determine how to hunt him. I would scout the area to find where the big bucks were staying. There are a few ways to determine how big a deer you are hunting might be. You can look at the bedding area of the deer or the size of the rub on a tree. However, the best way might be to judge the size of a buck by his tracks.

When I first started deer hunting, I would try to slip up on a buck. It takes a lot of patience and skill to do that. It is the most challenging way to take a buck. I can say I jumped many bucks before I ever perfected the stalking technique well enough to take my first buck, which was a nice 8-pointer. With a lot of practice, you can learn by doing the same as I did. I was able to kill several 8-point bucks using this method. I took one 9-point buck with a twenty-two-inch spread, twelve-inch tines, and weighing two hundred seventy-six pounds using the stalking method.

The day I took the 9-point buck, the wind was blowing in my face at fifteen to twenty miles per hour. I was hunting in lime rocks and was stepping from one rock to the other. I stopped on each rock to look out ahead. I had already taken some nice bucks before using this stalking method. Earlier that day, I had spotted some coyotes. So as I was walking, I was looking out for them too. I suddenly spotted the coyote moving through the woods at 150 yards away. I started moving very quietly, running from rock to rock, to try to get in position to shoot the coyote. In this process, I jumped up on a big rock, and this monster buck jumped up out from between two big rocks, not 20 feet away. I shot the buck at 30 yards. What an exciting way to take a monster buck! The 9-point buck weighed 276 pounds.

As I learned new methods of hunting big bucks, I found out that a big buck is going to be in the thickest cover he can find with an escape route near. So I started hunting in the thickest cedar tree and pine thicket area I could find. I would cut pine needles up and put them in a garbage bag with my hunting clothes. I had more confidence in this kind of scent cover than in any other I had used. I would find the thick cover in the woods, climb up in a cedar tree, and sit on a board that I had cut out to fit on a limb of the tree. The board was only about a foot square, but it was big enough. I would take my rattling horns made from deer horns that I had killed earlier and rattle them about every twenty to thirty minutes. I found out if I could get close to a thicket without spooking the deer, I could rattle and bring the deer to me. I have taken some big bucks using this method. I also rattled in some monster bucks that either came into the area from my back, or came in so fast I could not get a shot. It was still fun and exciting even if I didn't get a shot.

One Saturday morning in late December, I was in a cedar tree using the rattling technique. It was around eight o'clock in the morning, and I had been rattling for an hour off and on when a big 6-point buck walked out right in front of me. I knew that I was not going to shoot this 6-point buck, so I observed him looking back into the thick cedar thicket. I picked my horns up and clicked them together. The biggest buck I had ever seen raised his head and moved though the thicket. I was desperately trying to get a good shot on him, but it was too thick, and I did not want to take a chance of missing a buck that size. He looked like a mule—he was so tall! I was never able to get a good shot at him, so I had to let him walk. I was so excited about seeing a deer that size that I could hardly wait to get back to another hunt and have a chance of getting that big buck. I did not hunt the next day, which was a Sunday, but waited till Monday morning on New Year's Day to go after him. I was right back in that same cedar tree hoping to rattle that same big buck in again. I began rattling about seven o'clock, and then again about seven thirty, and again about eight. At eight o'clock, the 6-point deer came out and crossed in front of me just like on Saturday. Five minutes later, the monster 9-pointer came out of the thick cover and gave me the perfect shot. After I spotted the buck, it seemed like it was forever before he actually stepped into an opening that allowed me a clean shot at him. My heart was beating so fast. It was tough to hold my gun steady and have patience for the right shot. However, I mustered up my patience and waited until I got the perfect shot. I was confident that I had hit the big buck with my shot, but he disappeared into the thick woods. A few minutes later, I climbed down from the tree and walked toward the spot where the buck was standing when I shot. I immediately found the blood trail, tracked him about a hundred yards, and found him. I could not pick the massive 9-point buck up. I could not even move him. It took three people, with all their strength, to load that deer into a truck. I knew I had killed the buck of a lifetime.

I carried the buck to Blackwood's processing plant. We weighed the deer on the scales at the plant that was used to weigh all deer and calves they processed. The buck weighed a little over three hundred pounds. The rack was massive and is by far the biggest deer in weight that I have ever killed. I have killed many good bucks with more points, but none as big in size as this buck.

The most important first step in planning your hunt is scouting and knowing the area. Knowing how to access the area without spooking the deer is the second. The third is how to use the wind to your advantage. Over the years, I have found out that what you really need to have is patience. Being very selective in what you shoot is what makes a great hunter.

"The Big Buck," featured in the story of the
same name, surrounded by the fish featured
in "The Catch Before the Storm."

The Catch before the Storm

After graduating from Auburn and moving back to Blount County, where I was a teacher, coach, and farmer, I always looked forward every year to returning to Auburn for fishing in the spring and summer. The spring of 1976 was one to remember. My friend and I caught over one hundred pounds of bass in a two-day trip. He would not let us keep a fish unless it was over eight pounds, so I ended up with an eight, eight and three quarters, and a nine pounder. He ended up with two over eight. We released the rest of them back into the lake.

My friend taught me a lot about bass fishing. He was a biologist with a master's degree in bass habitat. I fished with him while I was a student at Auburn, and we caught a lot of fish during that time. On my first trip fishing with him, I tied a plastic worm on my line. He tied a crank bait on his line. He caught three seven-pounders before I could get my worm back to the boat! I said, "Hey, show me how to fish that bait." Ever since that day, I always have a crank bait tied on one of my rods and reels.

On one occasion, while students at Auburn, we went fishing on Chambers County Lake. We caught fourteen bass over five pounds during a three-hour period. The biggest was a nine-pounder that was caught by my friend. We were under a severe tornado watch that morning, but were catching these bass standing from the bank by throwing top hog spinner bait around tree tops. The day before, he had caught three over nine pounds, and had his line break on another.

I have always enjoyed taking my cousins and friends back with me on fishing trips to Lee County Lake. I believe every one of them has ended up with a bass to mount on their wall. One of my friends had his reel jerked out of his hands into the water, and he did not get his fish. I had a crank bait on my rod, so I made a quick cast to snag his line. I pulled the line up until it got to the rod and reel, and then I pulled it to the boat. Since he was using my rod and reel, I was happy that I was lucky enough to be able to retrieve it back out of the water.

On one trip, I caught several big bass, including one that was ten and three quarter's pounds. My friend that was with me on this trip asked me if he could borrow one of my fishing lures that I was catching my fish on. I told him I had a lure that I would loan him, which would catch a nine-pounder, but not one that would catch a ten-pounder and beat me. Of course, I was joking with him. By luck, with the lure that I loaned him, on the third or fourth cast, he caught a nine and three-quarter pound bass. I also had another friend watch me catch several six to eight-pounders on another day of fishing. I told him he would get his one chance to catch the big one, and late in the afternoon he caught a ten pounder.

In the summer of 1976, we had a two-man tournament on Lee County Lake for publicity for the lake to draw customers. During the time that we were students at Auburn, we fished this lake so much and caught so many big bass that we both had a point on the lake named after us and put on the map of the lake. Mr. and Mrs. Mullins, who ran the lake for all those years, had been so nice to my friend and me while we were students at Auburn that we agreed to help them out with some publicity to draw fishermen to the lake. I will never forget what good people they were and how they were such a big part of my life and the fishing at Lee County Lake. The memories of the visits and the fun I had talking with them are still some of my best memories. It was never the same for me going to Lee County Lake after they had to leave for health reasons.

The Mullins called the newspapers to cover the tournament that would be going on between my friend and me. Several people had watched us throughout the day, and were there at the weigh-in late that evening, along with the writer from the Auburn-Opelika News. The Auburn-Opelika News covered the story and wrote an article about the tournament. What a day of luck, I won the tournament with three fish that weighed a total of twenty-seven pounds. Boy, after that article, the next week a lot of people were on the lake fishing.

During the spring of 1993, I was looking forward to the spring fishing trip. That year would be a lot of fun because the whole family was going. My wife reserved us rooms in Auburn for several days. My daughter was playing in the All-State Band, and the state basketball tournament was being held at the coliseum. My son and I planned to fish Lee County Lake, and attend the Warrior versus North Sand Mountain basketball championship game. I had an interest in this game because North Sand Mountain had beaten us a few weeks earlier in the first round of the state playoffs. The Warrior coach had been up to school to visit me earlier that week, and we worked on a game plan for him to use in the game against North Sand Mountain. So I had a big interest in the game.

On Thursday morning, my son and I got up early so we could be on Lee County Lake fishing at daylight. It was a beautiful morning, warmer than usual for a March day. The water was perfect, with a slight ripple, and the wind was blowing out of the west. The skies had some gray clouds in the east, with a beautiful sunrise, and some red clouds mixed with the gray ones. This was a sign meaning a front may move in during the next few days.

We had planned to fish until ten o'clock and then go watch the game between Warrior and North Sand Mountain. We did not know what an exciting and historic day it would be. I headed straight toward Earl's Point, a place that had been named after me while I was a student at Auburn because I had caught so many big bass off that point. By this time, I had fished Earl's Point for over twenty years and knew every inch of the bottom and the cover. It was a long point that ran way out in the lake, with a knob that was located right at the end of the point. I put my anchor down right on top of the knob in four feet of water. I was in a position to cast in fourteen feet of water. I would cast my crank bait out to the deep and pull it hard until I hit the bottom, then let it float up for a second. That's usually when the hit occurred. If the bass hit, I would have to set the hook hard to penetrate the hooks into the big bass's mouth and get ready for the excitement of landing the big eight to ten pound bass. If that did not work, I would throw a nine-inch blue or black worm.

I had two methods of fishing the worm. One technique I used was to slowly move the worm, making it crawl on the bottom, stopping about every foot. The second was that I would jump the worm off the bottom with a twitching motion. I would try to concentrate on the steepest cut in the side of the point and work it first. The wind was out of the west, and the ripple on the water was perfect. I always said, "When the wind was out of the west, the bass would bite the best. When it's out of the north, they bite like a horse. When it's out of the east, they bite the least. And when it's out of the south, they bite like a mouse."

I was hoping my son was going to catch a big bass on that day. He got some bites, but he could not set the hook hard enough to land the big bass. It was not long before I had hung into my first big fish and had it in the boat. I caught this fish on a chartreuse crank bait. It was over eight pounds, and it was a good start for a great day. In a short time, I had another fish on my line, which was also over eight pounds. Right before ten o'clock that morning, I caught my third bass over eight pounds. It was hard to leave, but it was time to go to the game. However, catching three bass over eight pounds had made for an exciting morning.

At ten o'clock, we left to go watch the championship game between Warrior and North Sand Mountain. It was one of the best games I ever watched. My son still to this day says that was the best game, and one of his best childhood memories. Warrior won the game in overtime 103 to 102. Immediately after the game, we headed back to the lake. We were there by 3:30, with great anticipation of catching more big bass, not knowing what a great afternoon of fishing it would be. Within fifteen minutes after getting back on Earl's Point, I caught the biggest fish of the day, a ten and a half pounder. Five or six casts later, I caught the next fish, which was a nine and a half pounder. At that point, I was shaking from all the excitement. I had never caught a nine and ten pounder back to back. Then, I caught two over six pounds, which I released. The last fish of the day I caught was another eight pound bass. What a historic day of fishing!

I had caught a lot of fish before, but I had never caught eight bass over six pounds in one day. I kept the six bass over eight pounds and had them mounted. Two eight-pounders, an eight-and-half-pounder, an eight-and-three-quarters, a nine-and-a-half, and the ten-and-half-pounder—all hang on one wall in my house today as a reminder of the once in a lifetime catch I had that day.

On Friday, we heard a big snowstorm was going to hit north Alabama. It was seventy degrees in Auburn and people were walking around in shorts. It was a beautiful day and did not look like there could be any snow. We called home and asked if it was snowing. The family said, "Yes, it had just started." We happened to have our car and truck in Auburn, so I made the decision that my son and I would head home in the truck that afternoon. Halfway home, close to the town of Harpersville, I hit the snow. Within thirty minutes, I was driving in four inches of snow. I sure was glad I had a four-wheel-drive truck. We could only drive about thirty miles per hour because the snow was falling so fast we could barely see the road. By the time we got home, two hours later, we had eight inches of snow. The next morning, we had the historic snow of seventeen or eighteen inches. We did not have power in the house for a week. I had to keep the house heated with the wood heater to keep the pipes from freezing because the temperature dropped to single digits. My wife and daughter were not able to get home from Auburn until the next Wednesday. The snow was not supposed to reach down to Auburn, but it did. By late Friday night, Auburn had several inches of snow. It took about a week for the snow to melt, and the next weekend, I returned to Auburn for another exciting weekend of fishing. I caught twelve bass over five pounds, with the largest being seven and a half pounds. The fish were not as big as the bass I caught before the storm, but it was a lot of fun. The weekend of fishing right before the storm made history with the biggest catch of bass and the deepest snow in my lifetime. What a historic weekend to remember. I will never forget that big catch of bass the day before the Blizzard of '93.

Fishing Lee County Lake at Earl's
Point, named for the author.

The Comeback Win

As a young boy, I was always ready to go fishing. Growing up, my friends and I mainly fished the rivers and creeks for catfish. I would hear stories from my cousin about catching bass out of his grandpa's pond using a rod and reel, which sounded very exciting and new to me. I had always fished with a trotline, bank hooks, or cane poles on the rivers. I wanted a rod and reel, so I purchased one with some of my hard-earned cotton-picking money.

I got out in the yard and taught myself how to use my new rod and reel. I practiced casting a plastic worm until I could hit a spot on the ground with it. I begged my mother to take me down to my cousin's house so that I could go fishing with my new rod and reel. I had purchased some plastic worms because that was what I had heard my cousin had been using to catch the bass.

When I got down to the pond, the challenge of catching a bass on my new rod and reel was filled with excitement because this was my first attempt at bass fishing. I remember the beautiful setting so very well. Lily pads were growing thick on the pond. The lily pads had a few big gaps between them for a worm to drop down into the water. After fishing for a while, I made a cast, and my worm landed on a lily pad. I pulled it across to the next pad when a big explosion erupted at the top of the water. I let the bass have the worm for a second, and then I set the hook. I had hooked into my first bass, and within minutes, I had landed my first five-pound bass. I was hooked on a new way of fishing that would stay with me for life. I would continue bass fishing, catching many bass from this pond and others as a young boy. It became one of my most exciting and favorite hobbies.

Several years passed, and my cousin and I were all grown up. He had finished his service in the military, and had moved across the street from my wife and me. We were attending college, but found time to play Rook with our wives and get in lots of fishing. We caught a lot of fish that provided some good meals for us, as well as our family and friends. I remember we loved to go to the Mulberry River. We would set up all night and fish with our rods and reels. We would also put in trotlines on the shoals in waist-deep water, along with bank hooks hanging from limbs out over the deep water. This was a little risky, since there was a snake on almost every limb. We would shake the limbs, and the snakes would fall off into the water. Despite the abundance of snakes, we were not going to let that stop us from fishing.

I remember one night we caught a fish on almost every hook on one of our trotlines. We had also caught lots of fish using our rods and reels. We caught so many fish, we had to cut a pole and tie the stringer of fish to the middle of the pole. We got on each end of the pole, and the stringer of fish was so heavy the two of us could barely pick them up. It was difficult getting the heavy stringer of fish up the steep bank to the truck. I was so glad when we made it. By the time we got to the truck, it seemed like the fish weighed twice as much as they did when we started out with them. We had a lot of fun fishing, but it seemed like I was always the one baiting the trotlines and taking the fish off the hook, and my cousin was the one stringing the fish up. He was also very good at catching them on his rod and reel.

After a little more time had passed by, it was time for us to move to Auburn to pursue a degree in education at Auburn University. We made sure that we packed our rods and reels and our tackle boxes when we moved to Auburn. We did not know what good fishing we would find at Auburn. It was not long before I found a place to fish called Lee County Lake. We caught several six- and seven-pound bass from this lake. I caught so many bass off of one point that the people running the lake named it *Earl's Point*. I caught the lake-record bass from this point that weighed eight and a half pounds when the lake was only four years old. I spent a lot of time on this point, caught lots of big bass, and had lots of fun, some exciting times, and created many great memories.

When my cousin moved to Auburn, we spent a lot of time fishing the lake together. He was always watching the weather, which saved us from being caught in several storms and possibly from being struck by lightning. He was always worried about getting us to the bank safely before the storm hit, even though I always wanted to make one more cast, trying to catch the big one. When a storm was approaching, he had a saying: "It's time to head to the bank!" I did not heed his warning one day, and we got caught in a bad lightning storm. He never has let me forget that. He always had his tackle box organized neatly, and mine was always scattered all over the boat! He always had a Mountain Dew and a Snickers bar left at the end of the day. When all of mine were gone, I would ask him for a Mountain Dew. He was always reluctant to give me his last Mountain Dew. He would respond with, "What happened to yours?" These days, fishing is something we've been able to talk and laugh about many times over the years.

We would go to a store named Howard Sporting Goods to buy our fishing lures and supplies. This was where I bought my first Ambassadeur reel. We had to spend our money sparingly because I only made twenty-seven dollars a week while working at the vet school. I remember the salesman saying, "If you oil this reel, it will last you a lifetime." He was so right because the reel is still good after forty years. We were catching some good largemouth bass out of Lee County Lake and had learned how to catch four and five-pound spotted bass on Lake Martin. These four and five pound spotted bass could fight like ten-pound largemouth bass, so we needed a good rod and reel to be able to handle them.

On numerous occasions, even though it was a bit crazy, we would put a twelve-foot aluminum boat on top of a 1960 green Ford Fairlane and drive it forty miles to Lake Martin to fish the dock lights at night. The car had 260,000 miles on it, but it was all we had to drive. On one occasion while driving the old Fairlane to fish at Lake Martin, we had a flat on the front right tire. We were very fortunate to have the flat close to a filling station, which had a sign that said, "We fix flats." I walked up to a man in a rocking chair who was sitting in front of the station. Being happy to find someone to fix our flat, I asked him with a smile if he could fix our tire. He responded, "There are the tools boys, fix it yourself."

I proceeded to fix the flat, and the man only got up long enough to go inside and get us a patch, which, at that time, cost about a quarter. After I got the flat fixed, I asked him how much did we owe. He said, "That will be five dollars, boys." I paid the man but griped about it all night long while we were fishing. I sure was glad that as a young boy in high school, I had worked at a filling station fixing flats and pumping gas, so I knew how to fix the flat. I would say that the man had the perfect job: collecting the money after someone else did the work. Now, I knew what the sign meant when it said, "we" fix flats.

On Friday evenings, we would drive up to Lake Martin late in the evening, fish all night, and drive back the next morning at daylight. It was tough driving back the next morning with the sun coming up, thinking about all the studying we had to do when we got home. We would usually have to stop, wash our face, and get a Mountain Dew to drink to keep us awake until we got home, but boy did we made some good memories on those trips.

We always liked to make our fishing trips fun by making it competitive. I would usually beat him catching fish, which caused him to spend a lot of time netting and pulling fish that I caught out of the water. On one of our fishing trips to Lee County Lake, the fishing was tough, and he was beating me, four fish to three. He definitely had the upper hand, and the day was coming to an end. Our competitions would always end when the lake manager sounded the horn, which signaled for fisherman to exit the lake. With ten minutes to go, I knew I needed one fish to tie. I was really trying hard. I was concentrating, using my mind to think positively that I was about to catch a fish. With only a few minutes left, I got a hit on my crank bait, and I said, "Get the net." I knew he dreaded to net the fish that would tie the contest, but it was the honorable thing to do. Then I realized this could be a big fish, so I said, "Get the net! This is a big one!!" I got the fish to the boat, and my cousin used the dip net to bring in the fish—which was not one fish but two! I had caught two bass on the same cast using only the one crank bait. One of the bass weighed three pounds and the other one was four pounds. The horn sounded, and I had won our competition with five fish to my cousin's four. In all my years of fishing before and since, I have never again been able to catch two fish on the same cast.

After my cousin and I received our degrees in Education, we moved back to Blount County to start our teaching careers, and of course, we continued our fishing. On one cold March day, on a trip to Murphree's Lake, we had fished all day without catching a fish. It wasn't until ten after three when I finally felt a light tap on a blue worm. I set the hook hard, and after a great fight with lots of excitement that included seeing the fish up on top of the water shaking his head looking like a monster bass, I got the fish to the boat. My cousin put his hand into the mouth of the bass and lifted this ten-and-a-half-pound monster out of the water into the boat, helping me to get him in. On another occasion on Lake Manor, I caught a ten-pounder, and he lifted the fish into the boat for me again. I appreciate him lifting all of my big fish in the boat and keeping us safe from storms and lightning over our many years of fishing together. I cherish the memories we have together and for the adventure we had fishing. I will never forget my comeback win—the day I caught two fish on one cast. I remind him of that quite often, and he reminds me of the day I got us both caught out in the lightning storm.

The author's daughter, Deanna, examines
the catch of the day with her father.

The Guntersville Fishing Adventure

This is a story about fishing Guntersville Lake. As a young boy, I did a lot of bass fishing in farm ponds. As a young adult, I wanted to move a step-up and fish the big lakes like Guntersville, Smith, and Inland, but I did not have a big boat needed for these big lakes. I had purchased a fourteen-foot aluminum boat to fish Murphree Lake and Lake Manor, but I could not afford a big bass boat to fish the big lakes. I joined the Bass Fishing Club, knowing that we would draw for partners, and hoped that maybe I would draw a partner that owned a big boat like a ProCraft or a Ranger boat. This plan was going well, and I got to fish several tournaments in big bass boats with the people that I happened to partner with. I would of course pay my share of the cost of the trip, but being able to use their boat was certainly a nice advantage when I was a young man.

One fall day at the bass club meeting, everyone drew for partners. We happened to have an odd number of people that day. Since I was the last one drawing, I was the odd person out, so I was not able to draw a partner. We had planned to have a tournament on Guntersville Lake, and we would be launching our boats from the launch in Pole Cat Creek. Since I did not draw a partner, I chose to fish from my little aluminum boat, which had a 6-hp Evinrude motor on it.

I knew that for this tournament, I would not be able to go out into the big open water and fish the river in my little boat. However, I knew that Pole Cat Creek had some weed beds and boathouses in the upper end of the creek, and those places are usually a great place to catch big bass. So I headed up to the back of the creek, which was where the weed beds were located, on the steepest bank. It had deep water, and I started throwing a big blade spinner bait around those weeds beds. It was not long before I caught a bass weighing over six pounds. That was a great start!

Not long after landing the six-pound bass, I caught another bass around seven pounds, and then for the final bass of the day, I caught another big bass weighing almost seven pounds. I got very excited because I realized that I might have enough to win the tournament. Usually, if you had twenty pounds of bass, you had a chance to win. At the final weigh-in, I had almost twenty pounds of bass, and I had won the tournament. I felt like this was amazing because I was by myself fishing in a small boat. Everyone else who had partners was fishing from much nicer boats, some of which had 150-hp motors that would push them to seventy mph. I felt very fortunate to be able to win the tournament.

On another fishing day in late November, after coaching our last Friday night football game, we had a big tournament on Guntersville the next day. I stayed up until about twelve or one o'clock, because as coaches, we always went over the game film after the game. Still, I had to get up early and be ready to start fishing at five the next morning for the tournament. Earlier in the week, we had drawn for partners. I was unlucky again and did not draw a partner. That was okay though, since I had already won the previous tournament while fishing out of my little aluminum boat. However, I did not know what would be in store for me on that Saturday.

We launched our boats at Brown's Creek, which was much bigger than Pole Cat Creek. I had planned that after the launch, I would head toward another creek called Beach Creek, which I thought would be very calm fishing from my 14 foot aluminum boat. All of the big bass boats launched, went under the bridge, and headed in the other direction for the big river. I headed up Brown's Creek, toward the power lines and the boathouses and across the water toward Beach Creek. A cold front was moving in on this November day, but we did not realize how strong the wind would be getting.

At daylight, the water was calm, and just a few choppy waves. I fished under the power lines and got a couple of hits, but did not catch a fish. I made my way over to the boathouses, and at the first boat house, I caught my first bass, which weighed over seven pounds. I began to think that maybe this will be a repeat of me winning the tournament in Pole Cat Creek earlier in the fall.

I noticed the wind had started to pick up, and the waves across Brown's Creek, which were headed in my direction, started white-capping. Quickly, I hit another boat house, casting my crank bait. I caught another bass around seven pounds. This all happened in the first thirty minutes of fishing. I fished beside a few more boathouses, with no luck. So I went back to the boat house where I caught my first fish, and on the first cast, I caught another big bass identical to the first one in size. I now have three bass close to twenty pounds in the first hour of the day, so again, I felt like I would be winning the tournament. However, by eight o'clock, I could see the water white-capping at about two or three feet high, and the water already was so rough it was making my little boat bounce up and down. The wind and water were blowing in my face so bad that the rest of the day was not spent fishing, but simply trying to survive. The water got so rough that all I could do was to put my boat behind a boat house, and tie it up for protection from the waves. I could not get out in the deep open water, so all I could do was hang on and try to stay inside the little boat. The weather was so bad it made fishing impossible. I was waiting and hoping that the wind would let up before the end of the day so that I could make it all the way back across Brown's Creek, which was over three miles, in my little 14 foot aluminum boat with a six horse Evinrude motor. Weigh-in for the tournament was at five o'clock that afternoon. At two thirty, I realized that the strong wind was not going to stop, as the waves were three to four foot high, and the water was white-capping so badly that when you looked across the water, the top of the water actually looked white.

As the afternoon of rough weather continued, I knew it would take me over an hour to make it across the more-than-three-mile distance of rough water. I started out about two thirty, heading for the boat launch, and I saw that it was going to be very dangerous. My little boat with my six horse motor could barely move against the strong waves. I had to keep the boat at the perfect angle when I hit the waves because if the boat got at the wrong angle, the waves would turn me over. Heading into the big waves, my boat bounced so hard that my tackle box was bouncing in the bottom of my boat—and my bottom was bouncing in the seat! Even with my hat turned backward, the wind was about to blow it off my head. No longer am I thinking about winning the tournament—only about getting across the lake alive.

About halfway across Brown's Creek, the waves seemed to be at the worst, and for about twenty or thirty minutes in the middle of Brown's Creek—I didn't think I was going to make it! I did have my life jacket on, but the white-capping water made it very dangerous. I never thought about turning around and going back to the boathouses, because going with the waves would just make it more dangerous. So I continued holding my boat at the perfect angle against these white capping, dangerous waves. About three-fourths of the way across Brown's Creek, I saw that the waves were getting smaller because the road was blocking some of the wind. As I drew closer to the boat launch, the waves continued to get smaller. I realized that I was going to make it, and my thoughts changed from thinking I was going to turn over in that little 14 foot boat to thinking that I might actually win the tournament.

I arrived to the weigh-in by four thirty before all the rest of the boats arrived. When everyone in the big 17 foot bass boats with 150 horse motors arrived, they were complaining about what a rough day it had been and how dangerous it was to be out there fishing on a day like today. My only comment was, "You should have been in a 14 foot aluminum boat with a six horse Evinrude motor!" After all the talk about how dangerous, cold, and rough the water had been, it was time to weigh the fish to see who had won the tournament. I felt like I had a good chance with my three fish. Most boats did not even have a fish to weigh. I had 3 fish that weighed a little over 21 pounds and won the tournament! I still have that trophy in my trophy case today, along with the memories of overcoming unbelievable weather conditions and danger to win that day. I did learn my lesson not to ever try fishing Guntersville on a windy day like that again!

The author displays a stringer of bass, one of many
caught over his years of fishing adventures.

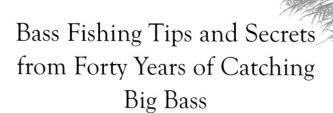

Bass Fishing Tips and Secrets from Forty Years of Catching Big Bass

Everyone has always wanted to know from me: How did you catch that big bass? What did you catch it on? Where did you catch it? I have heard these questions many times and I am finally ready to share my secrets of how to catch a trophy fish. I will do my best to tell you the secrets I have acquired through experience over forty years of fishing for trophy bass.

Having patience is key number one. However, having patience but fishing in the wrong place will not do you any good. Learn how to fish a few places well, and spend your time in productive locations. I usually tried to find five good places on a lake, and I learned how to fish those places well. Using this method, you can spend your time fishing in places where you have a high level of confidence and familiarity. Based on the time of year and weather conditions, each place may be better than others. For example, in the spring, bass will move up out of creek channels to steep points. In the fall, they might be on a big slope or point. So, knowing when and where to fish is a very important factor in being successful.

I have always heard that ten percent of the fishermen usually catch ninety percent of the fish. With today's technology, it has definitely made it easier to locate fish and catch them. In the past, we had to learn how to find fish the hard way, without all the fish locaters and sonar available today. In the past, we used our anchors to measure the depth of the water to find the points. We would move the boat along slowly, letting the anchor down to find the drop-offs on the edge of these points. A friend of mine from Auburn, who was a fisheries biologist, taught me to keep logs of every fishing trip. I would record things like air and water temperature, barometric pressure, weather fronts, the direction of the wind, the phase of the moon, and time of year. Of course, the time of day and date was always at the top of the page. These records really helped me plan my trips from year to year.

For most people, it is simple for them to decide when to go fishing. That is to say, they go whenever they have the free time. However, I will tell you the times and the seasons when I have had my biggest catches. Fishing during these times has proved to work year after year for me. In general, when the buds are full on the trees, but before the leaves bloom out full in the spring is always a great time to fish. Also, another great time to go fishing is after five consecutive days of no rain, and with the temperature above 95 degrees in the middle of June, preferably during the second or third week. Typically, after July 1, in the heat of the summer, finding and catching big bass becomes more difficult. However, once the heat of summer has passed, the third day after the first cool nights of late August or early September is always a prime fishing time. Also, another great time to fish is in the fall of the year, right before a hurricane or other low pressure moves in from the Gulf. If the hurricane, tropical storm, or other low pressure system moves east of the fishing site, then it will be an outstanding day for fishing. This was always one of my favorite times to fish, and when I have had some of my biggest catches.

Now in the spring, for the weather to warm up, usually the wind has to blow from the south. I like to fish the first day during the spring when the wind changes from the south and starts blowing from the west, hopefully on the third or fourth day after a warm up in the weather. Remember in the story, The Big Catch Before the Storm, I said that the big bass bite the best when the wind is out of the west. Now to catch big bass you must first locate the place to fish by finding the longest point that runs the farthest out in the lake with a steep cut slanting toward the west on that point, then fish facing the west on this steep slope. A slope that has access to deep water is the best place, and the steeper it is the better. If the wind is blowing bait fish into the point, the bass will be bunched up on the side of the steep cut. Sometimes, I could catch the bass right before I got my bait to the top of the point. If there is a hump on this point, that is even better. It is super if the slope facing the west has some cover on it like stumps and brush.

Before fish locaters came out, I would fan cast the point from the deep to the shallow, just as I would fish along the banks of the lake to find fish. If I caught a fish, I would mark my spot with a marker (fishing buoy), and I would then go find the shallowest place on the point, within casting distance of the buoy. That is where I would anchor down. It was sometimes difficult to cast into the wind, but that is what I wanted to do. I felt that positing my boat and casting into the wind did not spook the fish as bad, because the sound you made in the boat was being carried away from the fish by the wind.

When it comes to casting, make a long cast and pull your crank bait, or nine inch worm, into the slope, going with the wind, and maintain your bait in contact with the bottom. As you reel, concentrate on your bait coming up that slope. This is how I fished 75 to 80 percent of the time. Sometimes I would also work a jig or spinner bait from the deep water into the slope, especially if the slope had some cover on it. If I already knew how to fish the point, and thought it held big bass, I would sometimes skip the fan fishing technique to locate fish, and go straight to the point and anchor down. This is how I caught my biggest stringer of bass and some of my biggest fish.

After the leaves get full on the trees, the bass will move to the shallow water for bedding. Typically, the bass will begin to bed once the water temperature gets above 60 degrees. They will be scattered out, will become more easily spooked, and harder to catch. You will only have a short window of time to catch these bass around the bank before they go on the bed. If you do hit conditions right, it could be the catch of a lifetime.

In June, when it turns hot and dry, it will bunch the bass up in a tight area. To me, the mid-afternoon with the wind blowing hard was the best time for me to catch these bass bunched up tight. The hotter it was the better. I found fish in two places on these occasions. If you are able to find the fish, you can load your boat in a short time. I would fish over the top of underwater islands that were around nine to fourteen feet under the surface, or I would fish a ridge along the edge of the creek channel with sharp drop-offs. Again, the wind needs to be blowing against the cut or slope to push bait fish into it. Once I located the fish with crank baits by catching a bass I would then anchor down. I have been able to catch lots of bass in an afternoon using this technique. After they stop hitting crank baits, I would slow it down and fish a worm and most of the time continued catching bass. On the big lakes like Lake Guntersville when they are pulling water at the dam, all of the sandy gravel bars and underwater islands along the river are a super place to fish, and have produced some big catches for me.

As I mentioned earlier, the third day after the first cool nights in August or early September has been some of my best fishing times. I noticed this pattern early in my life while keeping my fishing log. I had one of my best fishing trips after an extreme cool snap in the last week of August. A friend and I caught a hundred pound of bass in one day, on the third day after the cool snap hit. In my log, I noted that we consistently had good luck fishing after the first cold snap of the year. We would catch these fish bunched up tight in the same places they were in for the summer pattern. However, the fish would be a lot more aggressive. We realized that shortly after this cold snap, the fish would move to the fall habitat, like the long shallower points.

In the fall, if you ever get a low pressure system moving in with lots of clouds and wind, it will be a different kind of fishing. From my log, I noted that if it was August, I would catch them on the same summer pattern. However, if it was September or October, I would need a different strategy. I loved fishing the spinner bait with a triple hook and a pork rind trailing. I caught a lot of big fish off shallow points and banks during this time of year. I also like the slues if the wind is blowing the water back up into these areas, especially if the slues have stumps and weed beds. In the slues, I love to fish the steepest bank, or the one with the most cover.

However, when all these techniques fail, it is time to try something new. It is time to experiment, to learn how to fish new baits, and find new locations on the lake to create some excitement. I can usually catch fish on any bait, any time, and in any location on the lake if I can find the fish. The key, and sometimes the challenge, is locating the fish!

Sometimes bass fishing can be a tough challenge, but it is always full of surprises. For example, one day I had fished all day without so much as a bite. However, right before I left to go home, I caught a ten and a half pounder within one hundred yards of the boat ramp. That was the only fish I caught on that day. This goes to show, in bass fishing, anything can happen at any time.

To answer the question about what baits were used to catch my big bass, I have caught bass over ten pounds on several different baits, such as nine inch worms, crank baits, spinner baits, jigs, and top water baits like jitter bugs. Bait presentations should change with the seasons. I think the presentation of the bait to the fish in the strike zone is more important than the type of bait used. However, if I could only pick one type of bait to fish with, it would be the nine inch worm. I like black worms with chartreuse tails on cloudy days, and a blue worm on bright sunny days. I will on occasion fish the worm on the bottom using a slow crawl, stopping every foot or so. I prefer jumping the worm off the bottom using two or three quick twitches of the tip of the rod. I like doing this in a rhythm, then letting the worm fall back to the bottom and sit still for a second. Big bass love to hit bait when it has stopped for a second, or when it's falling back down to the bottom. In addition to using the worm along the bottom, I have also caught fish swimming the worm on top like a snake.

My second pick of baits would be the crank bait. I like chartreuse sides with a dark top. However, the color does not matter as much as the fact that the bait needs to be big, have a tight wiggle, and be able to dig the bottom at nine to twelve feet down. My friend at Auburn taught me a trick on fishing crank baits that has helped me put many big bass in the boat. Cast as far as you can, and hold the rod tip down next to the water to get the bait digging the bottom as fast as you can. Whenever you get the bait to the strike zones, where you know the fish are holding on a point or a cut slope off the point, stop the bait from digging the bottom and let it float up, and that usually is where the strike will occur. If you do not get a strike, start digging the bottom again, but stop the bait about ten feet from the boat and let it float up again, then bring it to the boat. I have caught a lot of fish on this last stop before the bait gets to the boat. If you are fishing cover such as brush and stumps, bounce the bait off of them. This is where a good plug knocker comes into play to retrieve your crank bait if you get hung up on something. With practice, you can learn how to work crank baits through trees and brush without getting hung up very much. However, you have got to get the bait into the cover and bang it around a little in the fish's strike zone. I have caught five bass over five pounds each in about twenty minutes using this technique. On another occasion, I caught three bass over seven pounds in just a few minutes.

On a spring or fall day when the wind is blowing hard to give you some cover from the fish, a big double bladed spinner bait, buzzing right under the surface, has produced some big catches for me. Conditions have to be right, because I have pulled spinner baits for hours while not getting a strike, only to then find a bank with fish on it and have fun the rest of the day. I have caught bass over ten pounds on all the baits that I have mentioned, and as I think back, the biggest factor is where you throw your bait, not the bait you pick. I think the presentation of the lure to the fish in the strike zone is the most important factor in catching big fish. Most of all, the bait that you learn to fish well with and have the most confidence in is the one you will have the most success in landing your trophy.

The lakes I have fished are located all over Alabama. I have fished the big lakes like Guntersville, Smith, Lake

Martin, and many others. I have also fished the state lakes of Alabama, with Lee, Chambers, Monroe, and Dallas County lakes being my top picks, even though I have enjoyed some good catches on the other state lakes. I have fished some private lakes which have also provided some outstanding fishing. In one of these private lakes, consisting of about 120 acres, I caught five bass over nine pounds in one week while fishing before and after school. Now that's my kind of fishing! I like fishing lakes the size of a large pond up to about four hundred acres. These types of lakes are my pick, mainly because of the peaceful environment, where you don't have the hassles that occur on the big lakes.

I have caught big bass using many different fishing techniques. However, one of my most exciting catches was in the lake at my house, when I caught my first eight pound bass with my bare hands. I had an eight pounder strike at my thumb while I had my hand in the water after feeding some bass by hand at my lake. I caught her with my bare hands, but I quickly released her back in the lake. That was fun!! I now have pet bass in my lake that come to the pier for me to hand feed them, with the largest bass being about nine pounds. Now that I have turned them into pets, and feed them out of my hands daily, I can catch eight and nine pound bass anytime with my bare hands. By doing this, I have observed their behavior, and learned a lot from watching these fish. They are a lot smarter than we give them credit! Feeding these big bass out of my hands in my lake has been the most rewarding and enjoyable experience of all my bass fishing adventures.

I hope what I have written about my techniques of fishing for big bass will help you. The questions on how, what, and where hopefully have been answered. I have tried to the best of my ability to answer the questions I am most often asked by other fishermen. I have successfully caught big bass consistently over the forty years of my fishing experience, and I hope that my knowledge can be passed on to help you in some way that will assist you in catching your trophy. Even with today's technology, maybe some of my experiences will help you put your trophy in the boat. I am sure some of my tricks I used may still work today and may come in handy if you want to catch big bass.

Good luck fishing for your monster bass. I hope you will enjoy bass fishing as much as I have over the years.

The author, holding a bass from the lake at his home.

The author's parents, Roy Chester "Buster" Woodard and Annie Mae Woodard, in the garden behind their home.

Way Back When

As I get older, I think about the way it was way back when. I think about the simplest parts of life. My most cherished memories are my mother and granny working in the kitchen, preparing three meals a day. Oh, how good that food was, which they fixed from the food we grew in the garden or harvested from the land. I think of how nice it would be to go back and have one more meal that my mother and granny fixed. I think back to the house I grew up in, where a quilt was almost always hanging up on frames in the living room. Knowing how much time and work went in all those stitches that it took to make that quilt makes me appreciate it that much more today. The finished quilts were so beautiful, and would keep us warm at night for many years. I have fond memories of my grandmother working at the spinning wheel, and I always thought how fascinating it was to watch her work and make all the things by hand that were used in the house. I remember watching mother sew and patch all our clothes, especially our worn out blue jeans that she patched over and over. We wore the knees out crawling on them picking vegetables and playing games. Today, people actually buy faded blue jeans with holes in them. Ha! What a change. We could have provided them with plenty of jeans that had holes in the knees in our day.

As a boy, I remember walking along beside Papa Woodard with his mules, and trying to walk every step of the way with him. When he passed, a lot of the old ways passed with him. My dad taught me to plow a mule early in my childhood, and how to drive a tractor the day we got it. I think back to all the valuable things my dad taught me in his life and wish I could talk to him today. He would love to see my air-conditioned tractor!! He would be so proud.

Many things from life growing up on the farm often come back into my mind these days. Jumping up and down in a wagon filled with cotton, trying to pack it down so you can put more on the wagon was so much fun. Running barefooted through the fresh plowed dirt, and jumping in the river for a swim after a hard day's work was so rewarding, and was a part of our way of life. Finding a watermelon in the cotton patch while picking cotton, and busting it open and eating the heart out of it were the things that I did that this generation has missed.

The hunting, fishing, and adventures that I did way back when will be remembered through the stories that I have told and the stories that I have written, and will be passed down through generations for others to enjoy. I certainly enjoyed every minute I spent in the woods, on the rivers, and on lakes creating those memories. This was a part of life that was a necessity back then to provide food, but it later turned into a hobby and provided us recreation. Hopefully the stories can live on to be told or read for another day. Even though times were hard, we did not realize it because we were happy and loved our way of life. We took a little and made it go a long way. Most of our neighbors had the same type of life, so we all had a lot in common. Those were the days when neighbors farmed and helped one another and a man's word was his bond.

My parents had it hard living through the Great Depression. Both my father and my father-in-law served in World War II. After the war, they witnessed the most changes and greatest progress in American history. They lived through some of the hardest times, but also lived through some of the best times America has seen. As a teenager, it was fun listening to the neighbors discuss if we put a man on the moon or not. There were some of the older folks who believed we just landed in the desert and not on the moon. Although I knew that America did land on the moon, memories of neighbors discussing the issues of the day stand out in my mind today.

I remember sitting on the porch at night watching for the first satellites put into orbit. It was very exciting when we spotted one moving across the sky at night. In Papa's life he went from walking or riding a mule to cars passing by and planes flying in the skies. He also lived to see satellites orbiting the earth to watching America put a man on the moon. So what makes me think that it was the good old days? The way that families worked together on the farm, developing a closeness, helps to bring the memories of those from my generation back to that time.

Hopefully, reading the stories in this book gives an insight into the way it was back when, which is something this generation and the next will never know or experience. As a person gets older, their mind returns to their childhood days. For me, those days were a pleasant time in my life. I have seen many changes in my life, and I love all the modern conveniences and the present time I live in, but it sure is nice to go back and think about the best parts of the way life was way back when.

Epilogue

I wrote this book to preserve a way of life that has passed and will never be returned to. I hope my short stories will give the reader a feel of the way it was growing up back then. The changes that occur as one travels through this life are many. However, the principles of conquering the changes and challenges back then and now are the same. These are the principles that were taught to me early in life by my parents as a young boy growing up on the farm. Hard work, doing your best, and never giving up are at the core of these values. Many of these stories tell of the way I met these changes. Some of the stories are filled with adventure, excitement, and danger. These are some adventures we created to entertain ourselves because that was all we had to do. It was a time before television, computers, and modern conveniences. I do not recommend that anyone attempt to try any of these things I have done because it is unsafe and dangerous. One person said, "I don't see how you are alive." It was by the grace of God looking over me each day. Even though I was a country boy, I was able to fulfill all my dreams of becoming a teacher, coach, and farmer. Now I have retired as teacher and coach, and returned to my roots of doing what I was raised to do, which is being a country boy and a farmer. These stories may be viewed differently through someone else's eyes, but this is how I remember the stories and how I leave my stories to my family as I lived them.

RR2 Blountsville al
35031
205 429-2883

WOODYRD.ANGUSFARMS@gmail.com

3B3047206